T0128538

BUSKERS

BUSKERS

The On-the-Streets, In-the-Trains, Off-the-Grid Memoir of Two New York City Street Musicians

HETH WEINSTEIN and JED WEINSTEIN

Soft Skull Press

Library of Congress Cataloging-in-Publication Data
Weinstein, Heth.
 Buskers : the on-the-streets, in-the-trains, off-the-grid memoir of two New York City street musicians / Heth Weinstein and Jed Weinstein.
     p. cm.
 Includes bibliographical references and index.
 ISBN 978-1-59376-412-8 (alk. paper)
 1. Weinstein, Heth. 2. Weinstein, Jed. 3. Street musicians—New York (State)—New York—Biography. I. Weinstein, Jed. II. Title.
 ML420.W358A3 2011
 781.66092'2—dc22
 [B]
                                  2011011249

Cover design by Sharon McGill
Interior design by Elyse Strongin, Neuwirth & Associates, Inc.
Printed in the United States of America

Soft Skull Press
New York, NY

www.softskull.com

In consideration of their privacy, the names of some of the people appearing in this book have been changed. The timeline has been condensed for clarity and continuity.

To our mom

CONTENTS

INTRODUCTION

In the Shadows

[HETH]

'd been eating ketchup sandwiches for days when I drifted into the sanctuary of a midtown church to warm up and regroup. I needed to think things through, to figure out my next move. I was about to lose everything, including my apartment, my girlfriend Hope, and my two cats Jack and Milo, who were my kids. I hated that I'd become a broke-ass failed musician, presumably one of the world's worst providers.

Insert musician joke: *What's the difference between a pizza and a guitarist? A pizza can feed a family of four!*

The Midwest tour I'd just played with my current band had netted me exactly nothing, and now I was an out-of-work drummer on a mean losing streak, freezing my ass off, making the usual rounds, dropping off waiter applications anywhere and everywhere, with zero results. Restaurant managers must have found it impossible to overlook my severe lack of enthusiasm.

In the midst of this hopelessness, it took me a moment to notice the artistry of the stained glass windows or the rumbling of the hundred-year-old pipe organ. The church organist was in deep concentration practicing Mozart's *Mass in C Minor*. I knew the symphony from my childhood—the direct result of playing too much "Guess the Composer" on long family car trips with my music-obsessed parents and younger brother Jed. My brother and I were definitely the only kids on the playground who knew the difference between Vivaldi and Handel. The music echoed through the cathedral like it was Madison Square Garden. Steeped in the tranquil atmosphere of the church, my panic subsided as the vibration of a passing subway train rumbling beneath the wooden floor gave rise to an idea. I immediately raced back to my apartment and grabbed my gear. Within minutes I was trucking down the frozen steps of the Lexington Avenue subway station, ready to take my first crack at busking.

Half hallucinating, under the influence of low-blood-sugar delirium, I slid my guitar and battery-powered amplifier under the turnstile and jumped over it. From behind, I heard the clerk's muffled disapproval: "Pay your fare!" *Sorry token booth dude, can't this time. I'm saving up for a D19!* Earlier, I'd scanned Go Noodle's takeout menu for job-hunting inspiration, and the prospect of the delectably greasy D19—shrimp lo mein with soup and an egg roll—had me salivating as I rolled my equipment along the marble platform. I crammed my gear onto the train and rode one stop up to Seventy-seventh Street, just beyond Hunter College, where I'd often seen an old Asian guy playing recorder and doing pretty well. Hoping to emulate his success, I planned to set up exactly where he'd been performing.

Despite my desperation, I was self-conscious about my appearance. My thin black bomber jacket that had faithfully served me through several winters was now a shadow of its former glorious self. After several duct tape alterations, it resembled a Flash Gordon wardrobe malfunction. And there were holes in my jeans through which my long underwear was exposed, but not in that cool rock'n'roll way. My hair was longer than usual and pulled back into a ponytail. Today, I know buskers who try to look disheveled, using the tactic to grab the "pity drop." I don't blame them though; you gotta do whatever works for you.

After setting up, I nervously fastened the guitar strap to both ends of the guitar with fingers numb from one of the worst winters on record. Telling myself, "Dude, stop thinking, just play," I tuned up and flicked on the amp. The light by the power switch glowed yellow. Okay, all systems go. Time to play!

At the time, I was barely a guitarist, more like a drummer who desperately wished he could play the guitar. To skirt the need for years of lessons, I used an uncommon method of tuning that immediately enabled me to play a few songs, a kind of shortcut to competency. In this "open D" tuning, the neck of the guitar became similar to a keyboard, allowing me to form any chord simply by pressing the top two strings.

My awkward strumming wafted across the subway platform, surrounding me with confused, dense clouds of sound. As I played, I intuitively disguised the bum notes with my drummer's sense of rhythm, as if playing on beat would override my utter lack of skill. Whenever I caught a figure coming toward me, I assumed it was a cop or a station supervisor bent on my ejection. But after a few false alarms, I gave in and let the music take over, wearing my song like an invisible protective coat. Maybe that's why folks gathered around as they stood waiting for their trains. We were warming ourselves by the same fire.

I watched as my first underground audience assembled in front of me. People could have turned a blind eye, but a backpack-toting Hunter College kid led the charge, throwing a buck into my waiting guitar case. It was the start of a flurry of cash. More folks gathered, urging me on with compliments like, "Sounds great man!" and "Thanks for chilling me out." As the trains came and went, the ever-growing pile of my first busking dollars glowed succulently against the black velvet interior of my guitar case. With mounting excitement I realized I'd be able to make it through the month after all! As much as the cash meant to me, though, the compliments meant just as much.

A few hours later, I left the train station with a new job and enough money for fifteen D19s (looking back, I'm amazed I was able to perform uninterrupted for so long; the next couple of times I went back I was quickly thrown out). After years of struggle, I'd finally ascended to the level of professional musician, though in a way I had never anticipated. Why hadn't I done this sooner? I'm ashamed to admit that prior to my musical awakening, I shuffled through the city believing that only inferior musicians performed on the street. Gifted buskers unselfishly filled the city's public spaces with vitality, yet I'd been rushing by with scarcely a glance.

Triumphantly slurping lo mein and peering out of Go Noodle's window, I breathed a deep sigh of relief. For the first time, it felt okay that record companies hadn't appreciated me; I'd managed to bring my music directly to the public, regardless. But there was one more thing left to do. I had to track down my younger brother and ex-musical partner Jed and relay the news, in the hope he'd consider joining me again.

My thoughts turned to the pact we'd made ten years before: We promised each other we'd become rock stars together. For most of our lives, we'd had the kind of relationship other siblings envied. Maybe it was a result of sharing the same bedroom as kids, playing in the same rock groups, or simply surviving our father. For most of the previous two years, though, we had barely spoken. Our brotherhood had been annihilated by the bloody demise of our grunge band, Airport Hug. The trio we'd co-founded and lovingly nurtured from its inception had died a brutal death at the tender age of three. In band years, though, that's about fifty. We learned the hard way that bands are fragile organisms; few survive long enough to make even a second album.

As kids, Jed and I had been seduced by the magical early years of MTV (back when they played videos). All we wanted to do was rock! In an effort to join the lofty Day-Glo ranks of our musical heroes, we recorded demo after demo and sent tapes around to all the record companies. At first, there were some tentative nibbles, but ultimately nothing more came of our efforts than the standard rejection: "We hope you find a home for your music."

Undaunted, we maxed out credit cards, investing thousands of dollars to create and release our CDs independently. When all was said and done, we'd barely sold five hundred copies. By the time Airport Hug ground to a halt, our brotherhood and our finances had been pushed beyond the breaking point. We wondered if we could even breathe the same air again without kicking the living shit out of each other, and performing together seemed just as unlikely. The band broke up in true Spinal Tap form when I pressured Jed to ditch his girlfriend (also our acting band manager, and now his wife), who I was convinced favored him whenever it came to crucial band decisions.

Even so, I hoped to parlay my busking breakthrough into the excuse we needed to get back together. Over the last few months we'd begun to speak again, and now bit by bit we resurrected our relationship, growing closer, speaking on the phone and occasionally meeting for drinks at one of our favorite haunts, the Subway Inn across from Bloomingdales, where I first broached the subject of busking. Then, when the time was right, I invited Jed out for an early bird special in Little India, where, with sweaty palms and tail firmly placed between my legs, I blurted out over the Hindi music blasting in the background, "Hey man, I know I was a dick. I'm sorry about everything and hope you can forgive me." After an intensive heart-to-heart, I was relieved when we sealed the deal with a congratulatory high-five and a hug, and officially rededicated ourselves to our childhood pact to "make it" in music together . . . or die trying.

As we began picking up and reassembling the pieces, we had no idea what the future might hold, or how long we'd be able to maintain our fragile truce. We decided to reform as a duo, simply called

Heth and Jed, and resume our songwriting and performing partnership, the idea being we'd appear ninja-like in public places, ready to perform our songs. Both former skateboarders, we threw ourselves into the new gig like it was the X Games of street performance. Here was a chance to test our physical endurance while playing some of the gnarliest busking shows known to mankind, many lasting more than six hours. Today, after six years of playing in blistering heat and finger-freezing cold, tangling with police, drunks, crazies, and the roving gangs that attempt to dominate the city's prime busking real estate, our chops are so well honed that you could fire an RPG at us and we wouldn't miss a note. Over time, we proved the music industry wrong by selling tens of thousands of our CDs independently. More importantly, we figured out that while you may never reach the dream you hoped to achieve, with a little luck you might discover that the adventure was the ultimate reward.

1

Background Check

[HETH]

sually on the long subway ride home from a show, Jed and I are too tired to talk. We're wracked by thirst, tinnitus, and back pain. Though exhausted, we both intuitively scan the stuffy train car, easily reading the faces of fellow passengers, a survival skill that comes naturally to us now. I generally spend some of that time thinking about the events, seemingly random at the time, that brought me to this bizarre lifestyle.

Dad was my hero. He was also a natural comedian, often joking he was born at an early age to mixed parents—a man and a woman. *Ba-da-bump!* He loved quoting old Vaudeville shtick and was always ready with a one-liner. "My parents were so poor they couldn't afford kids . . . so the neighbors had me!" He'd been employed in the entertainment biz for most of his life, but by the time we were old enough to talk there wasn't much work available, and he could generally be found hanging out, getting high, and playing flute duets with his musician pals. As a result, our earliest memories are accompanied by a soundtrack of flute licks and metronome clicks, and interlaced with the pungent aroma of marijuana.

2

Sometimes we'd sneak in to his study while he was giving a flute lesson. Before kicking us out he'd take a minute to roll the metallic tasting flute against our lips. Dad patiently instructed, "Inhale. Exhale. Inhale. Exhale," demonstrating the precise angle at which exhalations become sound and little kids nearly black out from lack of oxygen.

Dad grew up in the Bronx, but just before his high school graduation his family relocated to sunny Santa Barbara, California where, against his parents' wishes, he joined a local mariachi band. At fifteen, he prided himself on being the youngest and only gringo in the group. When recalling those early days, he often joked that he wondered why the other guys in the group were always so mellow . . . until the day a fellow saxophonist gave him his first joint. When we were older, Dad bragged that he'd smoked grass back in the '50s when you could "blow smoke into a cop's face and the schmuck wouldn't know what it was."

One night Dad was the designated driver as the band made their way home from a show in San Luis Obispo. The fog was thick as they sped along the coastal mountain road. Nearing a curve, the guitarist sitting on the passenger side yelled, "Watch out!" The car skidded and screeched, coming to rest inches from the edge of a cliff. We owe our existence to that stoned mariachi dude.

After a gig, Dad typically walked into his parents' apartment high off his ass with Mexican music swirling in his head, only to find his parents just as he had left them earlier, sitting in the kitchen playing gin rummy. He said it would kill him if he ever ended up like that.

When I was five, Dad took a job with the Los Angeles Philharmonic. I remember tagging along with him to work. He plunked me down right next to him, surrounded by the full orchestra: woodwinds, brass, and timpani—the real deal. That was the first time I felt an honest-to-goodness surge of loud, unbridled musical power.

"Dad? How come you stopped playing?"

"See this?" he replied, pointing to a few squiggly symbols on the sheet music. "It's called a whole note rest. It means, don't play."

I fidgeted too much so eventually he moved me backstage and handed me a box of crayons, but not before a photographer from the *Los Angeles Times* snapped a photo of us. I was way proud when mom showed me the paper the next day—the two of us chilling together in the arts section for all to see.

Mom was an East Coast babe with a thick New York accent and attitude to match, but she loved California's perfect weather and easy-going vibe—a world away from her hometown. For most of our childhood she kept her dark chestnut hair waist-length, until she got the Jane Fonda shag and was consequently followed around Vons supermarket by people thinking she was a movie star (Mom swears she had it first).

While Dad taught us how to laugh, Mom made sure we were raised in a house where freethinking was always encouraged and racism considered an evil scourge. She came from tough but warm-hearted people. Her father Louis had emigrated from Russia and her mother Minnie from Poland, both making their way to America right before the master race began throwing Jews into ovens. Most of the men in her family were shit-kicking Marines, street-fighting guys who went from looking for trouble on Ninety-seventh Avenue in Queens to storming the beaches of Guadalcanal. Family legend has it that on our folks' wedding day, Mom's brother took Dad aside for a little "talk," making him understand that he'd kill him if he ever did his sister wrong. Dad knew he wasn't joking.

Mom says she was intrigued by Dad's wild side. Shortly after they first met in a philosophy class at Queens College, Ira and Carol (our parental units) were hitched and heading cross-country to Los Angeles in search of adventure. They settled in an area not far from Beverly Hills, where Dad's parents lived, taking up residence in an apartment building off Lincoln Boulevard that turned out to be a welcoming commune, an extended family mystically thrown together by the cosmos. The inhabitants of our little West Coast enclave were mainly students. Front doors were left wide open,

4

dormitory style, friends and neighbors dropping by at all hours to chat over a glass of wine. Since Mom was usually home with us kids, she ascended to the rank of unofficial chef for the premises, known far and wide for rare old-world specialties handed down from her grandmother, such as Hungarian goulash and lokshen kugel (essentially fried egg noodles with a cream cheese center). Our folks' dinner parties were ground zero for impromptu living room concerts, where a revolving cast of jazz and classical musicians gathered to jam. Jed and I crawled around our guests' feet while heated philosophical debates about everything from Picasso to the Los Angeles Dodgers raged overhead.

In keeping with the freakiness of the time, Hare Krishnas often turned up at our apartment asking for donations. To us, the sound of snapping finger bells and the chanting of their hit single, "Hare Krishna," was equivalent to the arrival of the Good Humor ice cream truck. We'd run to the window in anticipation of our barefoot visitors. They bunny hopped single-file along the alleyway leading up to our screen door, where we handed them oranges, bananas, and the occasional can of soup. After bowing graciously, they'd smile and without missing a beat of their mantra soldier on to the next residence. (Years later, these circumstances were reversed when Jed and I became the beneficiaries of a new generation's generosity: youngsters coaxed by their parents, waddling up to our open guitar case with dollar bills in hand, engaged in their first act of philanthropy.)

I wish those days could have lasted forever, but at the conclusion of Dad's stint with the symphony, our freewheeling California lifestyle came to a crashing halt. With no work in sight, he made the agonizing choice to move us east, where a job as cultural arts director for a Jewish community theater in West Orange, New Jersey, awaited.

Before we could even wave goodbye to the Krishnas, Jed and I were planted in the backseat of our '74 brown Dodge Dart with our cat Flippy, a bunch of kids' books, and an Etch A Sketch each, to keep us entertained. The speedometer read 110 MPH as Dad floored it across the open desert in the hope of getting us from one side of the country to the other before the car overheated. We didn't have air conditioning, so for thousands of miles all we heard was the wind beating in our ears and the radio blasting any jazz station Dad could dig up. With Flippy at our feet, we glanced out the back window to catch one last purple sunset dipping behind the Sedona Mountains. California and the closeness we shared with our father were officially about to become a memory.

AFTER A WEEK of sitting on our aching butts we arrived at 32 Lexington Drive—one in a row of nearly identical two-bedroom colonials in quaint Livingston, New Jersey, where the air was fresh compared to Los Angeles. Instead of lanky palm trees and hedges artistically manicured by Mexican gardeners, there were tall oaks, mow-it-yourself lawns, and an overabundance of American flags. The movers were days behind schedule delivering our belongings, so we spent most of our first week playing outside in the steamy August air and becoming well acquainted with humidity and our new surroundings. Mostly we hung out in the gutter of our barely traveled street playing Frisbee and popping the tar bubbles that blistered up in the baking sun, often getting sprayed with steamy plumes of tar juice. Those first few summers our clothes, shoes, and especially our fingernails were permanently stained black.

Our immediate neighborhood teemed with rug rats. Most every house on the block boasted at least a couple. This made for well-attended birthday parties and spectacular all-out neighborhood games of "kill the guy with the ball." If you were holding the ball, the last thing you'd see in your rearview before getting pummeled was the blur of a marauding pack of twenty little kids.

Though we loved hanging with our new friends, at times Jed and I missed the simplicity of California life. With our mellow outlook and sun-kissed shoulder-length hair it was clear we were ill equipped for the conservative North Jersey landscape. Wherever we went, people commented that Mom had "such beautiful daughters." To which we always shot back, "We're boys!"

We regularly pestered our parents, asking if we were ever going back home. "As long as we're together, we are home," Mom replied, trying to project her usual confident air. Somehow, we knew that meant never. So we resigned ourselves to making the best of it, especially when she shooed us outside, saying, "Get away from that TV set, it's going to rot your brain." That's when we ran into brothers Thomas and Niklas, who lived directly across the street. They were hard at work, digging shallow holes in their front lawn.

"Hey, what are you guys planting?"

"We're playing Holocaust," they robotically answered. "We're burying the dead Jews."

We shrugged and joined in, with absolutely no idea what the Holocaust was. When we were older, we found out Dad's side of the family lost a shit ton of relatives to the Nazis in Poland. A letter handed down to us in Yiddish and dated August 1945 gave us an eye-witness account of our relatives' last few seconds on earth. It read, in part: "[T]aken into the slaughter house, and slaughtered with the apparatus used to slaughter cattle." (Later on, Thomas and Niklas turned out to be pretty good guys, once they escaped the influence of their father, who'd shocked the town by writing a letter to the *West Essex Tribune* insisting the Holocaust never occurred.)

Biking around the neighborhood another day, we ran into a couple of older kids hanging out in the parking lot of 7-Eleven, just behind the high school. Our sweet Schwinn Sting-Rays were tricked out with prostate-friendly banana seats and had Vegas playing cards taped to the rims. As the wheels spun, the cards made a cool-ass clicking sound against the spokes, the kids' version of motorcycle vrooms.

"Hey, are you guys Jewish?" they asked.

"Yup," we replied. "Are you?"

Boom! One of them socked me in the eye and took off on my bike, leaving me in pain and Jed freaked out. A week later we found my mangled bike rusting at the bottom of Devil's Ditch, a swamp behind the high school football field, rims bent, banana seat nowhere to be found.

Then, during our first Jersey Passover, we ran into Big Paul, the undisputed king of our new hood. Everyone called him "Big" because he'd repeated eleventh grade an unspecified number of times, consequently towering over the rest of us. "What in the hell are you bagels eating now?" he asked, as we munched our matzo. Being avid fans of bagels, especially everything bagels with chive cream cheese, we didn't see anything wrong with the term, until that winter when all the kids from the hood gathered to sled down our street's big hill. That's when Paul and a few of his equally oversized pals tested out the results of their latest modification to the ordinary snowball: overnight storage in the freezer. As we whizzed by, they winged their ice balls at us, yelling, "Hit the bagels!" Of course I got nailed in the mouth on my first run. I freaked out when I noticed the freshly fallen snow at my feet turning cherry snow cone red. I abandoned my Flexible Flyer at the bottom of the hill, bolting home with Jed tagging behind me.

When we walked in, Dad took one look at my bloodied face and got a crazed look in his eyes. He dashed out of the house without even grabbing his coat. Thinking back, it must have been the street-wise Bronx kid inside him, or possibly the ever-deepening realization that he'd moved his family to Auschwitz, New Jersey. Either way, he totally snapped, marching across the neighbors' yards, making a beeline for Big Paul. Jed and I poked our heads out from behind a maple tree just in time to see him let loose with a tidal wave of violence, mashing Big Paul's face into two feet of powder, followed immediately by a knee to his nut sack.

Later that evening Paul's father came a-knockin'. I was pretty sure he wasn't finally getting around to welcoming us to the neighborhood. As the evening chill invaded our living room, I watched the two dads standing quietly on the porch, discussing the day's events. Jed and I overheard them saying something about not pressing charges, and that was pretty much that.

The next time we went sledding we sensed a palpable shift in local authority. With each successive run, kids parted for us like the Red Sea. As it turned out, Dad was a hell of a lot better at bullying than anyone in the vicinity. Readying at the top of the hill for yet another slalom, we looked up to see our parents on the front porch holding hands for one of the last times.

EVEN THOUGH WE saw Dad as our hero, a larger-than-life protector and watchdog, in real life the daily grind of office life slowly sucked the gusto out of him. He gradually stopped cracking his trademark slapstick jokes and patented one-liners like "Just call me Crisco for shortening." He barely played his flute anymore. When he did, he complained of his diminishing skill. "If you miss one day of practice, *you* know it," he theorized. "If you miss two days, *the band* knows it. And if you miss three, *the audience* knows it."

We'd seen warning signs: Mom crying alone in her room, and an inordinate number of secretive phone calls. Whenever the phone rang, Dad leapt to his feet and yelled, "I got it," then disappeared into the bathroom for hours, stretching the curly red cord to its limit. Other times, we'd answer a call only to hear a woman's mousy voice at the other end of the line taunting, "Ira doesn't love you anymore."

Finally, one day as we returned from a fun-filled excursion to the local Purim Carnival (a holiday celebrating Jewish victory over enemies), still equipped with groggers (noisemakers) and wearing King Akesh Varos costumes comprised of fake mustaches, Mom's costume jewelry, and gold paper crowns, our folks sat us down for a family conference.

"Boys, we have something to tell you," Mom began. "You've probably noticed mom and dad fighting a lot. It's by no means your fault, but we're going to be taking some time away from each other. Daddy is moving out."

Dad didn't say anything, only sported a weird grin, but we let out an audible gasp and fled to our bedroom crying, feeling like a nuclear bomb had just ripped through our home. Welcome to divorce, 1970s style.

Dad was having an affair with his secretary. At least that's how Mom eventually put it when she broke ranks and spilled the beans. Boy, was Dad angry about being outed. "The kids are too young to understand!"

Before the separation, and before we understood what "affair" meant, he had often brought his chiquita, Eleanor, by the house, playing her off as a close co-worker. Mom had even befriended her in hopes of smoothing our transition to town, hoping to reconstruct a new close-knit circle of friends for all of us, like we'd had back in California. We had played with her kids, who, incidentally, were pretty cool. But we certainly never expected any of this to happen.

Over time, we mostly adapted to the new arrangement, spending a night or two a week at Dad's new apartment, which was a giant hundred-year-old railroad apartment in East Orange, two towns away. But the neighborhood was so dodgy we were afraid to go outside, and we felt trapped and lonely for our friends and ever-expanding album collection. Dad must have thought the situation was about as permanent as a camping trip, because except for one brown air mattress, some sleeping bags, and a lone light bulb dangling from the ceiling, our bedroom remained unfurnished. Jed and I took turns either sleeping on the inflatable or sharing Dad's bed. At least until one of his psychiatrist friends said that would turn us gay, after which he evicted us like a couple of bedbugs and finally sprung for a second air mattress.

We blamed Dad's girlfriend for ruining our family. Everything came to a head a few months into the separation when we were walking with Dad by O'Neal's Balloon, a café across the street from Lincoln Center. Dad stopped us in our tracks, exclaiming in fake amazement, "Holy shit! Look who it is!" Eleanor had, not so coincidentally, commandeered a booth by the window. The plot to acquaint us with her charms was about to fail miserably. Dad made the mistake of dragging us inside to say hi, whereupon Jed let loose with the juiciest string of curses ever heard from the mouth of a nine-year-old on either side of the Mississippi. "You *fucking cunt! Goddamn bitch!*" he swore, giving her the one-finger salute, vibrating with rage. Dad tried to silence the little tyke by clapping his hand over his mouth, but to no avail. I dragged Jed outside into a nearby alleyway, assuming Dad would follow, but he never showed. We watched through the large bay window as he frantically tried to smooth things over with his paramour, with very little success.

As time went on, we began to hear rumors about Dad—that he'd gotten it on with neighbors' wives and even some local schoolteachers. Once-friendly adults turned cold. Even one of Jed's teachers vented her frustration over what I assume must have been an unfortunate encounter: "Mr. Weinstein! Sit down and stop talking! You seem to think you can get away with anything . . . just like your father."

It was Take Your Kids to Work Day at Dad's office when Eleanor finally cornered us for a little payback. "I'm telling you right now," she whispered. "I'm watching you little shits and this time I'm doing whatever I can to keep Ira away from you." She spoke Dad's name like she'd taken ownership.

For the most part, Dad was like a meteor hurtling past us from some distant galaxy, a stranger beaming in from time to time. But hey, at least riding in his car was fun. When he was baked, we often landed on someone's lawn or stuck in a ditch waiting for AAA. Like the time he volunteered to give a few of our friends a ride across town. He'd been entertaining us with one of his stories when our car did a three-sixty in the middle of rain-slicked South Livingston Avenue.

When we came to a rest, we cheered, "C'mon Dad, do it again!"

"No thanks," he said, maneuvering us back onto the road, eyes glazed from the Panama Red he kept stashed in the glove compartment. "Once is quite enough!"

When word leaked back, parents instructed kids not to ride with Mr. Weinstein anymore.

With Dad well on his way to starting a new family with Eleanor, Jed and I desperately tried to stay on his radar. The only place left for us to connect with him was at the theater he managed. The Maurice Levin Theater was a cozy five-hundred-seater where we gained a behind-the-scenes look into the lives of hardworking musicians. Dad took time from his busy schedule to introduce us to the Tokyo String Quartet, Martha Graham, and the Alvin Ailey Dance Company. We even hung with legends Peggy Lee and Buddy Rich.

One night, we snuck backstage and listened through the dressing room door while Buddy ripped into his band for most of the thirty-minute intermission. "What in the hell is wrong with you mother-fuckers?" he yelled. "What am I fucking paying you for?" He even threatened to replace the entire band by the next night's show if they didn't get it together. Apparently, the bitch-out sessions were so commonplace that the guys in his band took to secretly taping and distributing copies to their friends. I've got to hand it to Buddy: He was strict, but his band played the second set that night like they were on fire.

When we were old enough, Dad promoted us to ticket takers. That's when we became friendly with the audience—mainly wealthy Jewish retirees from Summit, Livingston, Short Hills, and West Orange, their names boldly emblazoned on the backs of the Playbills as "Patrons of the Arts."

They would kvetch, "Tell your father we need more Bach!" Or, "Please darling, tell him enough with the Rodgers and Hammerstein, already."

One guy in particular came to all the events. He never spoke a word, and with a faraway look in his eyes, he shakily handed me his ticket.

"Dad, what the hell is wrong with that guy?"

"Well, don't say anything, son," he made me promise. "But Mr. Goldberg's a survivor."

We wanted to be around Dad all the time, which is why the mornings after shows were always extra difficult. As the night's excitement dissipated, we were left deflated and bleary eyed. How could we be expected to concentrate on schoolwork after hanging with Sid Caesar or tagging along to Newark Airport to pick up the scary dude from the Brady Bunch Hawaii episode, aka Vincent Price? The world was obviously much wider than our little corner of it. Sensing our excitement, Mom asked what we wanted to be when we grew up. Our reply was always the same: "Musicians!"

But Dad, well aware of the hardship associated with living an artist's life, reached for one of his old standards, and with a faux Yiddish accent insisted, "Physician, not musician!"

2

Daddy's Weed

[JED]

I n a weird way, we welcomed our parents' separation. Before Dad moved out, we thought the normal state of family life was all-night screaming matches, punctuated by slamming doors and projectiles soaring overhead. Then, suddenly, there was stillness. A peaceful yet deafening silence blanketed our house. There was still the odd incident to liven things up though, like the time we walked in on Mom stabbing Dad with a pencil after he'd pushed her so hard she'd fallen against the kitchen stove.

Moments before the scuffle, Dad had dropped by the house for one of his frequent unannounced visits. He typically raided the fridge looking for remnants of one of Mom's specialties while multi-tasking a phone call to Eleanor. This time Mom wasn't having it and in an uncharacteristically bold move demanded he leave. During the ensuing attack, she defended herself with the nearest sensible object, a sharp Ticonderoga No. 2. Pop's vintage pencil sharpener became his undoing. That metal, desk-mountable Boston KS from the 1950s ensured that every pencil in our home was kept as sharp as a needle. In the end, he was left dazed, stumbling around the house with a bloody bath towel wrapped around his hand. Upstairs, Heth tried to comfort me with a hug as I sat crying in our bedroom. I whispered, "Why was Mom trying to kill Dad?" He didn't say anything, just squeezed me tighter.

Dad wasn't done with Mom by any means. While she was occupied at work, he'd sneak off with furniture and a smattering of valuable household items. Returning home from school, Heth and I often made a game of seeing who could spot what was missing.

"Uh oh, he got the painting from above the staircase."

"Yup," I replied, inspecting the dusty outline left in its place.

"Mom's gonna freak!"

Dad's next move was to empty the family bank account, thereby turning monthly child support into a political tug-of-war—with us kids stuck in the middle.

"Make sure you ask your father for the check," Mom instructed, dropping us off at his apartment for our weekly sleepover. She knew we were the best chance of getting him to fork over some much-needed coin. We'd agonize about when to broach the check subject for the duration of the entire visit.

"Dad, um, Mom wants us to remind you about the check."

Deep sigh. "I guess I should have known! The only reason you boys ever come here is for money. And besides, I just gave your crazy mother a check last week!"

The result? We frequently stared down the barrel of an empty fridge. As the noose tightened, Mom scurried around, maxing out credit cards and borrowing money from relatives, all the while looking for a better-paying job and a car that didn't break down every other week. Thankfully, after we applied to the School Lunch Program, the great state of New Jersey stepped in with meal cards— one for each of us kids. At least on weekdays we were guaranteed a hot lunch. Kind-hearted, hair-netted lunch ladies heaped extra-large portions of mac'n'cheese onto our Styrofoam plates while other kids looked on enviously. Still, they might as well have set up a siren in the lunchroom: "*Beep! Beep! Beep!* The Weinstein kids are poor. I repeat: The Weinstein kids are poor.*"

It wouldn't have been so bad if other students had meal tickets too, but the kids' side of our high school parking lot was filled with convertible Mercedes and BMWs while the teachers' side resembled a Pinto dealership. The rift between the haves and the have-nots was becoming increasingly clearer to us—especially at synagogue. On holidays we'd pull into Temple B'nai Abraham's elegant cul-de-sac in a rusted-out, poop-brown Dodge Dart. We'd sneak past the whispering crowds with as little fanfare as possible, clad in outdated hand-me-downs from relatives twenty years older, searching for a cozy pew in which to atone for our sins. We couldn't help feeling that compared to our impeccably coiffed peers, we looked like two adolescent disco kings in miniature elbow-padded leisure suits.

Mindful of our fiscal status, we gravitated toward kids in our own economic bracket, the ones who couldn't give a shit whether or not we could afford a school ski trip or a summer Teen Tour, the ones who could overlook the fact that our ailing front lawn (which everyone knows is the true measure of suburban affluence) had up and finally died on us, an outward manifestation of the disintegration of our folks' marriage. Anyway, all of us kids were quite adept at entertaining ourselves. After school, we'd often slip into the West Orange Water Reserve to have some fun, far behind the vacant fairgrounds. The grounds were off limits except for one week each summer when the local Kiwanis organization sponsored a traveling carnival. Just like the swarms of moths drawn to the flickering carnival lights, we were drawn to the intoxicating aroma of fried zeppoli and sausage and pepper heroes. There were all kinds of games, like the ring toss with rings that, of course, barely fit around the spindle. After losing a few bucks, if you complained long enough, the carnies would cave and hand you a few "win tickets" which you could redeem for cool shit, like a sparkly Lynyrd Skynyrd cocaine mirror or a glow-in-the-dark Jimi Hendrix poster. The best part was the rickety rides like the Twister that blasted KISS songs all night long. It spun like a top until the bottom dropped out and the centrifugal force nailed you to the wall. Kids always hurled on that one, so we made sure to watch from a safe distance. We could hear the commotion clear up to our house a mile away.

When the carnival left town, we'd all go back to trespassing, hiking through acres upon acres of lush unspoiled forest, a lost army brigade on a secret reconnaissance mission. Except for a few overgrown dirt roads where the game wardens prowled, checking water stations and looking for intruders, it was our paradise for miles, land just as George Washington and the colonial forces must have found it. Even so, we stayed on high alert. If they found us messing around back there, the wardens would hunt us down using air rifles, looking to shoot our asses full of salt pellets. No warning shots, nothing. Even though that shit stung like a mofo, we practically dared the wardens to chase us. It got our blood pumping.

For a brief moment, I too owned a gun. My pal Bobby King gave it to me for my twelfth birthday. It was a plastic hand-pump rifle that shot yellow rubber pellets. I tucked it into my bag and brought it along on an overnight stay at Dad's. But while excitedly showing him my new toy, I accidentally pointed the stupid thing in his direction. Before I knew it, he smacked me hard upside the head and took possession. Cracking it over his knee and throwing it at me he said, "See, that's what you get when you play with guns!"

It was stuff like this that had Heth and me treading carefully through Dad's world on constant lookout, trying to dodge his unpredictable, explosive temper. Sometimes, when he chased after us, we'd hightail it to the safety of the bathroom, the only room with a lock. We'd bargain, "You promise not to hit us if we come out?" Or we'd wait it out, hiding in the nearest closet, safely ensconced by musty-smelling haberdashery until he simmered down.

With Dad increasingly AWOL, Heth and I were beginning to look for outside parenting. Our best friend Ed was about our age, but had all the earmarks of an upstanding father figure: He could drink more beer than any of us and did the best burn-outs on his Mongoose BMX bike. He'd also grown up fast since his dad's death a few years earlier. In addition to his loss, his mom wasn't well, so it became incumbent upon fourteen-year-old Eddie to chauffeur her back and forth to work—something we respected. Beset with adult responsibility and difficulty seeing over the steering wheel, he made do, sitting on a stack of phone books. Once in a while he'd pick us up for a joy ride in his mom's fire engine red Yugo, and we'd hit the muddy banks of the Passaic River for some sweet off-roading. Good times!

His mom was a church organist and when the diocese purchased a new organ, they gifted her the old one. That thing was so humungous it barely fit in their living room. On special occasions, such as Christmas, she'd honor us with a command performance of classics like "Hallelujah" that had the entire house shaking—literally.

Mrs. O'Neil always treated us kids as equals. When making liquor runs she never failed to include us in the festivities, always returning with at least a few extra six-packs of Old Milwaukee for us. And whenever we cut school, she wrote the excusal note:

Please excuse Jed from class. He was ill.

Sincerely,
Mrs. Weinstein

For his fourteenth birthday she affectionately christened Heth "Space Cadet" and bought him a baseball cap with those illustrious words emblazoned on the crown. Heth's mind was always somewhere up in the clouds. People assumed he was a burnout long before he ever partied.

We appreciated Mrs. O's maternal ways, but what we really needed at the moment was some cold, hard cash. To this end, we had recently made a magnificent find. While cutting through North

Jersey Auto one day, the three of us discovered that the garage was leaving keys in the ignitions of the wrecks they were fixing. This gave rise to a plan. We returned later that night and made off with a banged-up piece-of-shit Toyota that made a heinous grinding noise anytime we threw it into gear (they should probably get that fixed). Before stashing it behind the racquetball club, we chugged up to "Sev" (7-Eleven) for the essentials: Coke Slurpees, Pixy Stix . . . and of course a few rounds of Defender.

The next morning we cut school, recovered the car, and headed up Route 280 to Dad's latest digs; a more kid-friendly apartment complex called Rutgers Village, located a town away in Parsippany. We took the Edwards Road exit, made a sharp left, and parked the clunker in Dad's lot. Then we snuck around the back of his building and hoisted each other through his office window. Once inside, we bee-lined it for the fridge, with Ed instantly taking charge of the sandwich making.

"Salameee! Salameee! Baloneee!" he said, quoting Bugs Bunny.

After pigging, we got right down to the business of rummaging through Dad's mothball-scented closet.

"See anything?"

"Nope, not yet," Heth replied. "Wait! What do we have here? Holy shit!"

"What is it?" I begged. "Lemme see. Lemme see." It was a Polaroid of Eleanor lying naked with her legs spread wide as the Grand Canyon. To this day we're still traumatized. There was something perverse about seeing the lady who had torn our family apart lying bare-assed on Dad's bed. The three of us fell silent as we took turns passing the X-rated photo around, joking that we should send it in to *Beaver Hunt Magazine* for entry in their "Amateur of the Month" contest.

Anyway, we were hunting for something more important. Where did he keep his cash? Unfortunately for us, Dad was apparently a fan of banks. But then Heth popped the lid off a nondescript shoebox at the back of the closet. Inside, we beheld not money, but a giant Ziploc bag overflowing with marijuana buds! There must have been at least a pound staring up at us, and the cherry on top was a large piece of what we eventually determined was a chunk of Lebanese black tar hash. Jackpot!

Heth cut up our booty into dime bags and sold it to kids all over town, using the proceeds to stock our fridge many times over. The first thing we bought was a case of cinnamon Pop-Tarts and a six-foot turkey sub with the works from Cammarata's Pizza Pantry. When the delivery guy showed up, we tipped him twenty bucks like a couple of miniature Pablo Escobars.

This was some grade A primo weed, not the usual North Jersey shwag. Because of its deep gold color we assumed it must be Acapulco Gold, a new strain we'd read about in *High Times* magazine. Most bizarre were the miniscule white crystals encrusted around each of the buds. We surmised this was some extraordinary plant biology, or maybe it was sprinkled with angel dust. Either way, it jettisoned our young brains into outer space. A mere toke or two caused hallucinations; three tokes and you could kiss the next five hours goodbye.

Our find was so potent that our good buddy John Cooper went momentarily blind after smoking it, complaining that all he could see was the color yellow. In disjointed sentences and broken syllables, he conveyed his wishes to be escorted from the woods where we were smoking back to the safety of our house for some peppermint tea. I'm not sure if it's an urban legend, but the scuttlebutt at the time was that drinking tea brought you down from a bum trip. Whether that is true or not, it's always a delightful beverage. Of course, after John was stabilized, we all smoked up again.

The locals had never smoked anything this strong, so demand was sky-high. Many times Heth would be sitting in class when seniors, who'd never before given him the time of day, dropped by, acting like his best friend. All at once we felt the magnitude of our situation. Either Dad's hallucination-inducing cannabis was poised to become legendary at Livingston High or we were going to be busted big-time. We felt our vulnerability keenly when a rogue kid named Alex Simmons tried to extort a decent amount of weed from us in exchange for not tipping off the police. We bought him off with a couple joints and explained that lots of kids, some of them very large, some of them on the football team, would not be pleased if they learned he was fucking with their dope supply.

Business continued unabated. We could barely get through a meal without the doorbell ringing.

"I'll get it, Mom!" Heth said, the budding entrepreneur happily rising from the table to greet yet another client.

In the end, we weren't afraid of Dad finding out we'd made off with his stash. What could he say? "Hey, did you kids steal my illegal drugs?" Our heist became the stuff of local legend and an unspoken secret between father and sons. Mom had retreated so deeply into herself from the pain of Dad's betrayal that she hadn't noticed our metamorphosis into low-end drug dealers, and while Dad was out spending money he'd inherited from an uncle who'd passed away, traveling the world with his girlfriend on his arm, we'd gone from guiltless little boys to pot-dealing delinquents hustling grocery money. From disillusionment to anger, from innocence shattered to hard reality. From "we have to rely on our parents" to "we're on our own."

WHEN THE WEED ran out we went back to our other pastime—shoplifting. What began as a way of putting food on the table had become an addictive rush. Our gang of friends lived by one simple rule: Steal at least one thing per day. Over time we came to regard theft as an art form, perpetually one-upping each other, testing our bravado and thievery skill sets in a never-ending quest for top outlaw bragging rights.

Our usual target was an unsuspecting supermarket that shall remain nameless. We customarily headed over to checkout, grabbed some brown paper bags, and then nonchalantly made our way up and down the aisles, filling them with whatever we fancied. It was like the show *Supermarket Sweep* where the contestants run amuck, grabbing items off the shelves willy-nilly. Once we'd checked off everything on our shopping list, we'd casually mosey out the door like paying customers.

If we couldn't sneak bags from behind the counter, we resorted to less inventive techniques, such as the underwear method. This involved nicking smaller items, shoving multi-packs of Velamints and Whatchamacallits (our faves) down our pants. The by-products of this technique were a wicked sugar high and an extraordinary bulge in the crotchular region.

With another eventful summer winding down and a new school year approaching, we needed supplies, so Mom took us up to Two Guys department store on Route 10 in East Hanover, basically a 1980s version of Kmart with everything from rifles, lawn mowers, and camping equipment to dollar-ninety-nine ELO records. Heth and I wound our way up and down the towering aisles slyly casing the joint like Baby Face Finsters. Though the interior was run-down, this store's security measures made our usual marks' efforts pale in comparison. We had no idea we were dancing with the big boys. To us little kids, the coast looked more than clear, so Heth made good on our "steal one thing a day" pact, stealthily shoving one of those newfangled erasable pens (like he really needed that item) down his pants. As we exited, store security nabbed him.

Ignorant of the circumstances, Mom shouted, "Let go of my son!" and yanked Heth toward her.

"I'll take it from here," Heth said, trying to cover his ass. "Everything's cool, Mom. You guys go on home and I'll meet up with you later."

Pfft. As if Mom was ever going to let that happen. Plus, we were like seven miles from home. They hauled Heth and Mom into the back room where they took his photo and added him to the "Banned for Life" corkboard. Ultimately, it wasn't much of a sentence, because they went out of business a year and a half later.

Some years after high school, we were invited to a party in West Caldwell hosted by someone whose family, unbeknownst to us, had owned the Two Guys franchise way-back-when. When Heth off-handedly made a comment about being caught stealing up there, the dude responded, "It's because of assholes like you my family went bankrupt! You know what? I think I'd like you to leave."

SINCE DAD HAD wised up and found a new spot to hide his stash from our grubby little hands, we were now forced to get our weed from other sources. One of our connections was a guy named Bill Clarke who was a dishonorably discharged Marine in his late twenties living down the block with his mom. Bill was the neighborhood acid casualty, a public reminder of what happened to those who strayed a little too far into the drug world. Sometimes he meditated cross-legged in the middle of our street, burning incense and chanting Hare Krishna mantras while wearing one of those folded newspaper pirate hats. His mom begged, "Billy, get back in here!" But he usually wouldn't budge until the police arrived.

Restricted by a permanently revoked driver's license, Bill was forced to walk from here to there. He'd walk for hours, sometimes to far-flung places. While driving with our mom practically in the next county, we'd see him off in the distance doing his unmistakable, bopping walk on the side of the road. "Holy crap! There's Bill!" we'd yell excitedly. "How the hell did he get way out here?"

A typical drug buy started with Bill walking the five or so miles to make a purchase from his secret supplier over in West Orange. On the way back, he'd invariably stop along the route to smoke as much of our product as possible. Then we'd meet up at "the logs," our regular party spot in what we called St. Phil's woods, the natural refuge of forest and fallen trees between our house, the high school, and St. Philomena Church. Buying an ounce from Bill meant we'd end up with a little over fifty percent of our order. Also, while couriering he typically stashed the bag in his underwear, in case the cops stopped him. This would have been fine, except he rarely showered. When he handed over the weed, the usually lovely pot aroma was overpowered by the scent of Bill's sweaty balls.

When we weren't partying at the logs with Bill, we found solace in Ed's bedroom, a veritable sweat lodge for psychedelic enthusiasts. We sat in each other's presence, lights off, incense wafting, all of us teenagers worshipping at the altar of almighty rock'n'roll, listening to everything from the Cars and the Clash to Black Sabbath, the Doors, Cream, Zeppelin and that intense, live Rush album, *Exit . . . Stage Left*.

We had bonded with a bunch of adventurous kids, a select group of partiers all bent on taking the same amazing, mind-expanding journey. Heeding Jim Morrison's plea to "break on through," we hoped for a glimpse of what awaited us in the afterlife. Like junior pharmacists in white lab coats we worked with dosage, discovering that with the right cocktail of illicit substances we could exist inside a Pink Floyd record, swimming in the colors and shapes the music radiated. To push things further, we gathered speakers from all the kids' houses and daisy chained them into an '80s version of Surround Sound.

One time we were listening to "Several Species of Small Furry Animals" off of Floyd's *Ummagumma* (a song that makes excellent use of the entire stereo spectrum), when Heth asked, "Dudes, anyone else seeing frickin' trails?" We'd been hipped to the "multiplying effect" in health class: If you smoked weed after drinking, you automatically doubled the high. Thanks for the heads up.

DNA AND SPLENDID drug supply aside, Dad had unknowingly aided our musical journey in one other way: He'd left behind a 1970s wood-paneled, tube-powered Pioneer stereo system, through which mythical New York City DJs Scott Muni and Carol Miller fed us a steady diet of rock'n'roll bliss. Our headphones were the umbilical cord connecting us to new sounds, new worlds, and, most importantly, other dimensions. The world felt beautifully sad when we moped around to the sounds of Joy Division, Ministry, OMD, and the Cure. We also slam danced to the razor-sharp power chords of two-minute punk ditties from the likes of Bad Brains, Flipper, the Dead Kennedys, and Black Flag, all the while avoiding disco like the revolting scourge it was.

All this time, the desire to make music was growing inside us like some irrepressible genetic disease. Heth and I were intent on forming our very own band as soon as possible. Actually, we'd been behaving like a band way before we could play instruments. Soon, to the further dismay of our neighbors, the cacophony of off-beat drumming and out-of-tune guitars replaced our parents' all-night screaming matches.

3

Our First Taste of New York

[HETH]

"**W**anna take a ride?" Dad asked, pulling up in front of our house in his new car.

"Hell yeah!" we replied, pointing in Ed and Adam's direction. "Can we bring our friends?"

"Sure."

He was eager to show off his new toy, especially the way it handled the S curves of South Orange Avenue—New Jersey's answer to San Francisco's Lombard Street. After a few passes, we convinced him to park so we could all go for a hike at nearby South Mountain Reservation, which was easily a couple thousand acres of unspoiled trails and fields.

At Campbell Pond I hopped out onto some rocks. Dad followed close behind but blocked me when I tried to return to shore.

"C'mon," I said, laughing. "What are you doing?"

He blindsided me, knocking me ass-first into the slime green, algae-choked water. Back on dry land I was shivering and embarrassed. "C'mon, motherfucker," I said, taking a few half-hearted swings at him and bracing myself for another smack to the head. When he connected, his punches felt like cement blocks smacking my brain loose. "Man, your dad's a friggin' psycho!" Ed whispered when it was over, as he helped me to my feet. As we silently rode home in Pop's sweet new ride, all I could think about was how someday I'd be able to kick his fat ass.

That opportunity presented itself half a year later, when I was a bit taller and had a little more meat on me. While practicing on my drum pad with the thick steel drumsticks I used for strengthening my wrists, I heard a commotion and ran upstairs to find him wrestling with Mom again.

"I can visit whenever I want to. I pay half the mortgage for Chrissakes!"

Mom was yelling, "Let go of me, you son of a bitch!"

"Dad, leave her alone!" I screamed, as I lodged my drumsticks under his Adam's apple and tried to pry her free.

We jockeyed back and forth, chasing each other around the dining room.

"Little boy's a man now?" he taunted.

Click, click, click, click. The metronome in the basement was still keeping perfect time when Dad stormed out of the house.

THE VIOLENCE IN the air followed me to my first year at Heritage Junior High. I had hoped for a smooth start to the school year but my excitement soured on the very first day when a huge ninth-grade jock named Sal Bruno took an instant dislike to me.

"Hey faggot! Nice hair," he said, impressing his entourage of chuckling meatheads.

As I walked by, he tripped me. I fell hard, then picked up my belongings only to have them slammed out of my arms yet again. All the other kids were staring at me and laughing.

After that, I tried like hell to avoid him but he kept finding me— near the metal shop, in the gym locker room, even on the way home from school. It was always the same: "Faggot," followed by a beat-down.

One day, I made the mistake of venturing down a barely used basement hallway by the art classrooms. I saw Sal off in the distance and hoped for the best as we walked the lengthy hallway like two gunslingers in a face off.

"Why don't you cut that hair, faggot?" he asked again.

"Why don't you suck my dick?" I replied.

All at once I completely lost it. I didn't care about anything anymore. You could keep my fucked up father and this whole bullshit existence. I wanted out of this world, but not until I made that steroid case bleed, and bleed he did when I struck him in his nose with a fast right hook. With blood gushing down his face he picked me up like a rag doll and body slammed me onto the marble floor. My head cracked down so hard you could have heard it clear down to the end of the hallway. After that, he pretty much moved on to tormenting other freshmen, but kept me as an alternate on his victim roster for when business was slow.

One morning, they made an announcement over the school PA. "We are very sorry to announce that student Salvatore Bruno was killed in a car accident last night. Our hearts and prayers go out to his friends and family." Some girls started crying and even a few of the guys teared up. Our homeroom teacher went over to comfort them while I sat there beaming, looking around the classroom for someone to high-five.

WITH MY HEIGHTENED tendency to violence I could now fly into a blind rage with barely any provocation, and this inevitably filtered down to my interactions with little Jed. I still feel bad about it. On several occasions, we spilled out onto the front lawn in full brawl, Mom running out the door alongside us yelling, "Stop it! Stop it! I'm calling the police!" We didn't care. As far as we were concerned, there wasn't much else we could do to embarrass ourselves in front of the neighbors, and fuck them anyway for having such perfect little lives. On the other hand, if anybody else messed with Jed I'd turn into his psycho protector, taking on kids twice my size.

When we weren't coming to fisticuffs with the entire eastern seaboard, Jed and I practiced our instruments relentlessly. Initially, sans drum kit, I made do bashing the hell out of mom's defenseless couch pillows and unsuspecting crockery, pretending to be Charlie Watts, the Rolling Stones' human metronome. Eventually I found out that a kid down the street had a sweet, green-sparkled Ludwig kit, so I decided to make him my new best friend. As it happened, Steve said he'd already switched over to guitar and "would rather practice his lessons with a live drummer over a metronome any day." It was the perfect arrangement, since I thought drumming was the coolest fucking thing in the world and it felt really, really good to hit something besides Jed.

"Hi, is Steve home?" I asked his mom, knowing full well he wasn't. "Well, would it be okay if I waited for him . . . in the basement?"

I couldn't wait to descend the stairs past the typical North Jersey sump pump into their mildewed basement and rip into that sweet drum kit for hours on end. Thankfully Steve's folks were tolerant of all the noise, his mom occasionally folding laundry down there while I hammered away. But I was well aware I was overstaying my welcome, so I tried prying a couple a hundred bucks of bar mitzvah money from Pops to purchase my very own kit—no small feat.

Before the internet and Craigslist, the most efficient way to buy used gear in New Jersey was through a rag called the *Want Ad Press*. With the latest issue in hand, I skimmed past the used cars and boats section, making for the holy pages of musical instruments. Most of the sets were priced well out of my league until . . . come to Papa: *For Sale. 5 pc. Slingerland drum set. All hardware incl. $250.00 O.B.O.* We cruised up to Butler, where Dad did an awesome job bargaining with the owner, an intimidating Hells Angels type sporting a cool looking Fu Manchu.

Sensing how important it was to me, Mom graciously allowed Dad on the premises for the watershed moment. At home, we assembled the $185 kit in record time, but just as I was about to mount my steed Dad jumped on the drum stool and started beating the skins. He'd often told us tales of drumming with saxophonist Gerry Mulligan in the Village and set about proving it.

"How about giving me a chance?" I begged.

Like a senator in mid-filibuster, he wouldn't budge, so after a while I gave up and dejectedly hiked over to St. Philomena's woods to wait it out. No matter how far from the house I went, I could still hear him bashing away.

It was torture sitting through class knowing my drum set was home alone just waiting for me. (Yes, I was one of those annoying kids who relentlessly tapped his desk with a pencil.) After school, while mathletes solved brain-melting equations and wrestlers played grab-ass in the gymnasium, I blissfully skipped home, walking straight through the front door to bid my baby hello. I drummed so much that piles of drumstick shards several inches high accumulated at my feet every few days. Drumming became my escape from the daily household chaos, and gradually my self-esteem grew as I excelled at something other than getting high.

When some kid at school mentioned it had been proven that the act of drumming summoned the devil, I was a little unnerved. It seemed plausible. At the time, we were watching a lot of movies about the occult such as *The Exorcist* and *The Omen*, while in the news, we saw Tipper Gore and the PMRC denounce our favorite albums as the root of all evil. I had questions. Did this mean I was risking demonic possession in pursuit of musical glory?

Nevertheless, I bravely secured a boom box to the bookshelf directly behind my head and painstakingly set about unlocking the mysteries surrounding every John Bonham drum lick, flam, and paradiddle known to mankind. I remember taking on the super-human "Good Times, Bad Times," a song in which Bonzo introduced me to the unnatural technique of using one's foot to hit rapid-fire, sixteenth-note triplets on a single bass drum. In an effort to become the "best foot" in North Jersey I worked my technique so hard that, over time, my right calf became twice as muscular as my left.

My kit, while in some disrepair, was good enough to get me up and running in my first band. By age fifteen, I was playing the cover band bar circuit up around Nyack, New York. I mainly remember being paid in beer and everyone being way older than me. Like father, like son.

In the meantime, with Dizzy Gillespie as his primary hero, Jed gravitated to the trumpet. Dad approved of this and sprung for lessons immediately. The two had bonded over jazz and formed the kind of close relationship I envied. Dad even spent time teaching him how to sight-read music, while I was stuck somewhere on the sidelines in firstborn purgatory. Learning from my example, Jed knew that once he grew a personality, the honeymoon between him and Dad would be over too. But until then, Dad was really there for him and took him to see Dizzy anytime he was in town. Diz invited kids up on stage at the end of every show, and somehow Dad always made sure Jed was up there.

Dizzy asked, "So what instrument do you want to play when you grow up, young man?"

"Trumpet!" he always answered.

Once after Dizzy performed in Washington Square Park with his big band, Jed asked him if they could take a photo together. Dizzy grabbed him and gave him an incredible bear hug while Dad squeezed off a shot with his Kodak.

Jed's trumpet teacher was a stuffy old Juilliard professor, the spitting image of Lawrence Welk. Mr. Treutel had taught such greats as Wynton Marsalis and Lew Soloff of Blood, Sweat & Tears fame (Lew was the one who rocked the classic trumpet solo on "Spinning

Wheel".) Jed excelled and was viewed as something of a young prodigy by his liege, at least until my friend Mike and I secretly inserted the nastiest porn spread we could get our hands on into his *Canadian Brass Book of Intermediate Trumpet Solos*—retaliation for the latest evil practical joke he'd played on us. Jed unwittingly handed the lesson book to his teacher who, upon opening it, got an eyeful of some California surfer dude sticking his gigantic tool between a massive pair of fake tits. "Hmmm, what's this here?" he asked, adjusting his bifocals.

In the subsequent weeks, Jed tried squeezing out a few more lessons from his instructor (carefully checking all his trumpet books for contraband beforehand) but was finally rebuffed, his teacher believing him to be some kind of twisted, low-life pervert. When Mike and I heard the details we hit the floor laughing so hard, we nearly pissed ourselves, then actually felt kind of bad about the whole thing.

PUBERTY WAS HORMONAL roulette. Some kids sailed through, developing muscles and enough self-esteem to run for class president. Others, like me, had zits and so much self-doubt I took refuge behind a pair of mirrored, psychedelic John Lennon sunglasses and an oversized, government-issued military jacket for the duration. It didn't help matters that Dad was always commenting, "Man, your face is looking pretty bad today." Yes, Father, thank you for alerting me to this fact.

But when he was in a good mood he'd take us on spontaneous adventures, often in New York City. On my fifteenth birthday, he picked us up after school and whisked us away for a greasy meal at his favorite Chinatown dive. The stench of industrial Jersey burned into our lungs like tear gas as we crossed the Pulaski Skyway making for the Holland tunnel. Jed and I customarily pulled our shirts over our faces, using them as makeshift gas masks, breathing only through our mouths until safely out of nose shot.

Our destination, Wo Hop, was the undisputed McDonald's of Chinatown cuisine. They'd been serving up legendary MSG-laced dishes in that dank, Mott Street basement for over five decades (and are still at it today). The decor was uniquely New York City, the walls plastered with signed headshots of local nobodies. It was also where the cops often ate, since the courthouses were only a block away. The other cool thing about the place, besides the time Chinese mobsters executed one of the cooks, was how the waiters kibitzed with you like you were family, asking all kinds of uncomfortable questions like, "How's that lovely wife?" obviously referring to Dad's new girl-friend. Jed and I left that one alone.

We ordered our favorites: chicken fried rice, spare ribs, egg rolls, wor shu op (fried duck), and wonton soup, the bowl overflowing with humongous chunks of pork and Chinese cabbage. Our MSG headaches already in full swing, we headed out onto the fishy smelling street to fulfill the other purpose of our outing: a meeting with Dad's fireworks connection, a mobster named Chinatown. (I immediately liked this guy for having the balls to name himself after the entire neighborhood.) The man could usually be found hanging around a parking lot on Baxter Street.

"Chinatown around?"

"Wait here," the parking attendant replied, sizing us up.

Moments later a disheveled goodfella materialized. Immediately dispensing with the pleasantries, he began selling the shit out of us.

"Okay gents, whaddya need today? I got Romans. I got fountains. I got some nice missiles and mines." (Not to be confused with military devices of the same name.) In spite of his mobster demeanor, Chinatown had an ethical streak, often mentioning he could get dynamite just as long as it wasn't for us kids.

We waited, trying to act cool, like we weren't from the 'burbs, while Dad once again bargained like a pro. Chinatown reappeared carrying a bulging red plastic bag containing several bricks of fire-crackers and a couple hundred bottle rockets. On the way home, Jed and I keenly inspected our gifts, running our hands over the lumpy packaging with the cool Chinese graphics. You could smell a hint of gunpowder through the bags. We felt like badass gunrunners as we drove west through the Holland Tunnel making for the Jersey line. Pulling into our driveway, we busted out of the car, eager to blow shit up with our friends.

With fireworks in hand, the true purpose of our house's ratty sunroof was finally revealed. It proved to be an exceptional launch pad for all-out neighborhood bottle rocket wars. The main goal of the contest was to pick off kids scattered around the lawn below. When a missile lodged in someone's hair (extra points for that, of course) the concussion from the blast could leave a kid temporarily deaf with a high-pitched *weeeeee* sound ringing in his ears. Our lawn looked like a 3-D reenactment of *Apocalypse Now*, complete with smoke, sulfur stink, and debris strewn about.

YOU CAN'T CONTROL outside circumstances. That's something Mom learned the hard way. She'd been outgunned and demoralized by Dad's slick divorce attorney, and following the proceedings, fell into serious debt. On top of the legal bills, the water heater and the washing machine broke, then the front steps fell apart, and then the roof needed to be re-shingled, all in rapid succession. We came home from school one day to find her crying in bed, short of breath.

"Mom, what's wrong?"

"I'm having a heart attack!"

"Oh my God," we replied in our usual brotherly unison. "Should we call an ambulance?"

"No, no, I don't want to go to the hospital!" she insisted, wriggling free from our grasp and plunking back down on her queen-sized bed, flanked by empty ice cream buckets, decomposing apple cores, and reams of completed *New York Times* crossword puzzles.

Upon further interrogation, she finally concluded it was merely a panic attack, but she sure had us worried.

Broke and convinced that our entire gossip-crazy town knew of Pop's infidelity, Mom could barely pull herself out of bed anymore. The prospect of running into any of his conquests at, say, ShopRite or Livingston Pharmacy was too daunting. Except for her 9-to-5 in customer service at *Newsweek* magazine, Mom was effectively a shut-in.

Alone and desperate to help her, we did the only thing we could think of. We watched and learned from the master himself. One windy spring night at 2 AM we stood lookout with Ed, while Ryan Miller, one of the biggest druggies in school and head Eagle Scout of local Troop 51, wrapped a towel around his hand and punched out the backdoor window of a quaint two-storey Cape Cod. Ryan was a tough army brat who enforced a strict code of "partying etiquette." Getting high with him was like being in druggie boot camp. We couldn't laugh uncontrollably or act too wasted or we'd be reprimanded. "Listen dude," he'd warn, using his tag line: "Calm your fucking hormones."

We had successfully gotten inside the house when my colleagues' faces started melting. I tried to remain calm, so as not to catch Ryan's ire, gently reminding myself it was merely a fine hit of primo acid kicking in. But the hit made my stomach hurt like there was an angry baby kicking inside. Then my tongue went numb along with my hands, leaving me wandering around the house like a blob of protoplasmic reticulum—something we'd recently studied in biology class.

LSD had come to Livingston High by way of our buddy Glen, a local kid who had recently returned from an illustrious stint as our high school's first runaway. After a month of living in the subway stations of New York City, he'd returned home holding ten sheets of supposedly killer blotter acid, each hit stamped with a tiny illustration of Snoopy snoozing peacefully atop his red doghouse.

My trip that night wasn't turning out to be particularly peaceful, and, in desperate need of some relief, I called upon his Dog-ness for guidance, envisioning Snoopy as my benevolent acid-trip spiritual guide. *Please, Snoopy, don't abandon me.*

We were in full-on psychoactive-fueled hysterics when we floated upstairs to the master bedroom of the cozy, middle-class home, whereupon we immediately located a wooden jewelry box on the dresser and began stuffing pillowcases full of the Richardsons' valuables.

"Holy shit!" Ryan said, rummaging around under the bed. "I just found their fucking adoption papers!"

"Those kids were adopted?" Ed asked. "Wow, I never knew."

A few minutes later, Jed was jumping up and down on the bed when he heard the distorted sounds of a police radio.

"Dude! Somebody's out back!"

But it was hard to judge sound. Noises were forming shapes.

"Pull your shit together, soldier!" Ryan commanded.

A neighbor must have called the cops. We heard one more garbled walkie-talkie transmission and that was it for us. We grabbed our loot and bolted down the plush shag-carpeted staircase at full speed. With feet wobbling out from underneath us, we all piled out the back door, shooting past the pigs like a pack of psychedelic gazelles, then disappeared into the familiar terrain of St. Phil's woods. Snoopy must have been with us, because not one of us got caught, but Jed and I stayed up all night tripping out and worrying. We were certain they'd forensically trace our footprints through the dew-soaked lawns, leading them directly to our front door. For weeks after, whenever the doorbell rang we thought it was the authorities coming to haul our asses to juvie hall.

To unload the goods, we played hooky from school, riding the 77 Community Coach Bus into Manhattan. After arriving at the Port Authority Bus Terminal, we trekked up Eighth Avenue into the cum-drenched heart of 1980s Times Square sleaze. This was

Forty-second Street before Giuliani—not a legitimate movie theater or Olive Garden in sight. Instead, a vast panorama of raunchy peep shows and porn shops stretched as far as the eye could see.

We weren't in Manhattan fifteen minutes when a guy asking for directions targeted us as suburban and turned mugger on us, making a gun shape with his hand underneath his Mets jersey. He advised, "I don't wanna blow a goddamned hole in my shirt so give me all your fucking money . . . NOW!" While the rest of us jumped into the street to escape, nearly getting rammed by a bus on Seventh Avenue, Ryan explained to our would-be assailant, "Bro, you ain't getting shit." The mugger looked stunned, then much to our relief took off running down the block. Yes, we were obviously a bunch of naïve, suburban high school teenagers, but Ryan was on a whole other plane.

After our auspicious welcome, we headed five blocks north to Forty-seventh Street and Sixth Avenue, looking to do some business in the diamond district. Noticing a giant, neon WE BUY GOLD sign, we nervously jogged up a narrow staircase adorned with flashing disco lights, whereupon two Chasidic dudes helped us turn a few thousand dollars of gold into four hundred dollars cash. None of us had ever seen that kind of money. We rolled out onto the streets like we'd just won the lottery—not to mention the relief we felt finally ridding ourselves of Exhibit A.

Afterwards, we celebrated by purchasing fake IDs and a few bottles of malt liquor, both without incident. This was amazing to me; back in Livingston, kids were always getting busted buying alcohol at the Bottle King, one of the only liquor stores for miles. (After this first trip, sensing a gap in the market, we regularly made the commute solely to fill kids' alcohol orders, returning with duffel bags full of beer.)

We were roaming Forty-second Street in the afternoon smog, eating hot dogs and admiring larger-than-life nude chicks adorning classic vaudeville theater marquees, when we noticed a video arcade.

Like a flock of rats led by the Pied Piper, we were lured across the street by the high-pitched din of Frogger, Asteroids, and Pac-Man all blaring into a mishmash of electronic fuzz—super-sweet music to our teenage ears. The arcade was thick with cigarette smoke and packed with intimidating inner-city kids wearing fedoras, unlaced Adidas, and Michael Jackson rhinestone-studded gloves—something we'd never seen up close. The game consoles had seen a lot of action too. Their plastic outer shells were dotted with cigarette-burn battle scars and the controllers were nice and loose, making them easier to maneuver.

We changed ten bucks into quarters, using eighty-five cents to purchase a pack of Marlboro Reds from the vending machine. "Butt me." That meant whoever had the cigs should hand one over. For a while we owned Missile Command, and then one of the coin guys spotted us sneaking sips of Schlitz Malt Liquor from brown paper bags and asked for identification. We eagerly whipped out our new IDs, keen to put them to the test, but that dude knew a fake from the camera store around the corner when he saw one, and we were unceremoniously ejected.

On the way home, we sat in the last seats of the bus discussing our good fortune.

Things were certainly looking up.

AS IT HAPPENED, Mom's fortunes were about to change for the better as well. A friend of hers had recommended a gifted therapist who incorporated a hefty dose of Vipassana meditation in his therapy sessions. We'll never forget how awkward it felt the first time we walked in on her in deep concentration, eyes closed, sitting cross-legged on her meditation pillow. We cracked up. Mom slowly opened her eyes and joined in, the three of us sharing a good laugh for the first time in a very long while. It was like she'd undergone some kind of Buddhist intervention. Sensing our curiosity, and secretly hoping he'd set us straight, Mom asked us if we wanted to meet Dan, her therapist.

Our first appointment was at his studio a few blocks from the Museum of Natural History. At the time, we were living life at full volume: pierced ears, camouflage pants, ripped-up Clash kamikaze t-shirts, and the requisite black combat boots. All we wanted to do was fight, rock out, and tell any and all authority figures to suck our fucking dicks, twice on Sunday.

But it was clear from the outset that type of approach wasn't going to work. During our first visit, Dan asked us point blank, "How does it feel to have a depressed mother and a father who doesn't give a fuck about you?"

That sure caught our attention. He didn't bullshit, and we liked that. He also cursed as much as we did, and we liked that too. We soon found out he was a serious badass, a dude who'd been a druggie, a soldier, and an artist among other things, until he spent a silent year alone, meditating in the mountains. Through self-imposed exile, he'd gained a deeper understanding of the natural laws of the universe.

What a sight it must have been, the punks meeting the monk.

"Let your eyelids close," he instructed, as we tentatively slipped into meditation for the first time.

"Concentrate on the rise and fall of your breath, sensing it wherever you feel it strongest. Let the breath move through you unhindered. You don't need to govern your breathing; the hypothalamus has evolved over millennia to do that for you. Notice the emptiness at the end of your exhale right before the body gathers the next breath, that's where a sense of timelessness resides. When you notice your mind wandering, let go of the distracting thoughts and gently return your focus to your breath once again."

After twenty minutes of concentrating, the room had heated up noticeably and our bodies felt weighed down by a heavy, balancing energy. All the while, I kept thinking how weird it was to be meditating in such a holistic setting around the corner from the Hayden Planetarium, where we sometimes scored acid before seeing Laser Floyd.

We began seeing Dan on a regular basis. He became an ally and a friend and encouraged us to begin a daily meditation practice. "Meditation is as essential as oxygen . . . and you two have been under water for a long time." A year after our first meeting, I had to admit I felt way more at peace. My anger level had diminished and I'd gone from a straight-D delinquent to honor roll student. Though by that time it was too late to look for decent colleges, I'd decided to get good grades simply to prove I could do it, and also to shake off some of the wastoid stoner reputation I'd acquired from all my years of partying.

By the end of high school, our penchant for crime was past, and music was the primary thing on our minds—one of the last links tethering us to our father's genetics. To this day we can still feel his DNA surging through us when we're playing a really smoking concert, or whenever we feel the impulse to hurt the ones we love.

4

The Great Escape

[JED]

"Hey, you guys party?"

"Sure do," we replied.

"Well, we've got some shrooms . . . if you'd like."

The voice was attached to a luscious blond babe—think Stevie Nicks circa *Rumours*. She and her friend had been sunning themselves, leaning against a celestially adorned Dodge hippie van with orange paisley window drapes and requisite dancing bear stickers, when we happened along. My brother and I hadn't known them fifteen minutes before we were in the back of their mobile love shack making out with them. Our new girlfriends balanced bits and pieces of magic mushrooms on their tongues, transferring the consecrated material to our mouths with each kiss. It was certainly the best tailgate party I'd ever attended.

Two hours prior to the mushroom make-out session, Heth had picked me up at San Francisco International. I'd suffered through a brutal People Express flight (a no-frills sky bus like JetBlue—only way more ghetto). After an emotional reunion, I was elated when big bro whipped out two tickets for the evening's festivities. We'd be attending the Grateful Dead Chinese New Year show at Kaiser Convention Center in Oakland.

"Holy shit!" I said, my heart skipping a beat.

As it had turned out, Heth hadn't needed to worry about getting into college after all. Ben, our parents' former Los Angeles landlady's son—and also our godfather—was all grown up, and currently dean of a college in Northern Cal. And his great spread in nearby Los Altos boasted a guesthouse where Heth could stay for the duration of his studies.

Over numerous long distance calls, Heth regaled me with amazing stories of the abundance of both the superior Humboldt County weed and the easygoing West Coast girls. I remember a collect call from Swensen's Ice Cream Parlor in Mountain View, where he worked as a scooper. Some smoking hot chick had walked in and ordered a chocolate-covered frozen banana. You can probably guess what happened next . . . She began sucking that piece of produce suggestively, stuffing it down her throat, making all sorts of slurping noises while staring him down. Then she leapt up off her chair and with a knowing smile, skipped out the front door giggling, leaving Heth alone with his boner.

"Dude, did you get her number?"

"Nope . . . I pussed out, man."

Later, she called the store asking him what flavor he came in.

I thought to myself, shit, maybe I should get a job at the Baskin-Robbins in Livingston.

It had been a rough few months prior to my visit. Not wanting to stress Heth out during his first year away, I kept Mom's mounting health issues secret. While he'd known about her routine hysterectomy, he had no idea she'd suffered in terrible pain for weeks following the operation. It struck me as unfair that therapist Dan had just helped her lick her depression, and now she was facing a whole different kind of hurt. The idiot alcoholic doctor hadn't tied off the stitches properly, leaving her with internal bleeding. When Mom complained, Dr. Steinberg played it down, saying it was common for females to overreact to pain. Eventually the discomfort became excruciating and she checked herself back into St. Barnabas where she endured an additional operation and two more weeks' recovery time spent in the hospital.

During that period, I was unaccompanied, fending for myself for the first time at the age of seventeen. Pops had promised to move back into 32 Lexington temporarily, but he didn't show. By the time my buddy Aaron pulled up on his moped I was in full-blown panic mode. The poor guy took pity on me, graciously offering to camp out until Mom was discharged or until his parents noticed he was missing from their humongous mansion, whichever came first. Mom still wasn't quite out of the woods yet but I didn't say anything to Heth. Best to concentrate on hanging with my brother, enjoying San Francisco, and having our minds blown by the Dead.

Dead shows were my milestones. How much had I grown since last seeing Jerry and the boys? What new events had shaped me? The nature of their music lent itself to introspection, especially during long Jerry Jams. Heth and I were used to seeing them at Madison Square Garden, but from up in the nosebleeds, far above all the action, amid the twirlers and whirling dervishes. The Bay Area Dead scene was hella different from what we were used to. For one thing, movement was unrestricted, so we easily deposited ourselves directly in front of the stage; back east security checked your ticket stub ten fucking times per show. And I practically had to rub my eyes in disbelief when, before the show, I noticed a volleyball game raging in the middle of the auditorium. I think it was the Bill Graham Crackers vs. the China Cat Sunflowers. The audience was mostly old timers who'd been seeing the band for decades, plus a smattering of us kids, the younger generation newly discovering their magic.

When the house lights dimmed, the vibe electrified. With the band keenly ripping into their party anthem "Hell in a Bucket,"

Kaiser shook and swayed as if enjoying the show as much as we were. Hell fucking yeah! The potent combination of jet lag and shrooms had me breathing under water, inhaling choice hits of liquid space music. Heth and I were exactly where we were supposed to be, in the Kingdom of Heaven, dancing to the good ol' Grateful Dead, surrounded by our newly adopted and ever-so-accepting surrogate family.

The Dead were doing what they do best, expertly surfing the room's energy wave as we cheered them on to higher levels of musical exploration. There were no negative vibes, just the ebb and flow of cosmic energy on a magical February night, twelve miles east of San Francisco, a million miles from New Jersey. The whole audience engaged in one communal moment of bliss, all of us passengers on the same asteroid, floating somewhere in the middle of the Milky Way Galaxy. That evening forever changed the way Heth and I perceived music and performance. Still, it would take several years before we were able to connect the dots.

ONCE HOME IN Livingston, I slipped back into the mundane relatively quickly, with only my new haircut to remind me where I'd been. Heth had shaved the sides of my head and given me a pretty rad Mohawk, topping it off with a few bright red and blue streaks. Friends liked it, saying it reminded them of a horse's mane, although a year and a half later, when I entered music school, it garnered a surprising amount of negative attention. Surely such a creativity-rich atmosphere would be hospitable to my freakdom? Nope. The jazz department of William Patterson College in Wayne, New Jersey was more repressed than a gay priest. Considered to be one of the best music schools in the country, William Patterson was often visited by big name musicians who came sniffing around campus in hopes of discovering the next young prodigy. One time, drummer Roland Vazquez did a guest spot with one of the student bands. A month later he invited a fellow trumpet player, only a sophomore at the time, to join his European tour. As a result, things became quite competitive. I remember how once-friendly kids turned malevolent, trying to psych me out whenever they had the chance, especially right before each important recital.

"Dude, watch your pitch!" Or, "Watch me for the cue, you keep missing the coda at the end of 'All of Me.'" All designed to destroy confidence. I fell for it, making stupid errors that left me frustrated and doubting my trumpet abilities.

To defend myself, I fell back on a little of the old Weinstein charm, informing Pete Ambrose, the biggest dick and pack leader, "Bro! If you say another fucking word to me or even look in my direction I will knock your fucking teeth out." This worked splendidly, but the school's faculty wasn't amused.

One day while making my way to class, I paused outside an ensemble room to listen in as Rufus Reid and few of the other esteemed professors jammed Miles Davis's *Kind of Blue*.

"Hey Agassi!" Rufus called, nicknaming me after the mullet-wearing tennis pro on account of my "crazy" haircut.

"Hey, Mr. Reid," I said, sheepishly poking my head inside.

What a site to behold. Rufus killing it on bass; Jim McNeely, a Stan Getz alumnus, on piano; and Steve Turre from the *Saturday Night Live* band on trombone.

"Get in here man. Let's jam."

Holy shit! My heroes were asking me to jam with them?

Three, four, five, and away we went, all taking turns soloing over Dave Brubeck's "Take Five."

For the next ten minutes the rehearsal room morphed into a smoky Fifty-second Street jazz joint circa 1959, and I discharged an arsenal of Lee Morgan and Miles Davis riffs I'd been wood-shedding all semester long. Holding my own amongst some of the best jazz musicians in the world, I believed I was finally ready for the big-time.

"Now tell me, Agassi," Rufus quizzed. "What's the last chord we ended on? Diminished, minor . . . augmented?"

"Umm, I'm not quite sure."

"But, you have to know."

"I don't know what it is, but I know how to play it. Doesn't that count?"

"Listen, as head of the jazz department, it's my obligation to give you a reality check. You ain't never gonna make it in music."

At first I thought he was joking. I waited in the hushed silence hoping for some kind of divine reprieve, but it never came.

"Well, I'm not here to make it in music," I said, regaining composure. "I'm here to learn about music."

Though only nineteen, deep down I knew he was right, at least regarding the jazz world. Jazz seemed to be an old boy network, an exercise in following rules and preserving the past, something I didn't want any part of. I further reasoned they probably didn't need a rocker dude like me lousing up their scene.

Driving home, somewhere around Ridgefield Avenue in Caldwell, with Hüsker Dü cranking on my car stereo, it dawned on me that rock'n'roll was way more accepting. All were welcome in its deafening room, earplugs optional—even fuck-ups like me. Correction: especially fuck-ups like me. And shit, I know when I'm not wanted.

Having recently read that Statue of Liberty poem "The New Colossus" in English lit, the words began running through my brain with a slight twist. "Give me your tired, your poor, your huddled masses yearning to *rock* free."

I'd been toying with the idea of dropping out anyway, since Pop's tuition checks kept bouncing. The next day I was analyzing a Beethoven string quartet in music theory class when it dawned on me how deeply I had fallen under Dad's spell. After all this time, I was still trying to get him to keep his promises and to recognize how much I loved him. But staring enviously out the window at a pack of Canada geese flying south for the winter, I wondered how I was supposed to give a rat's ass about tonality and melodic inversions when I had the added complication of the bursar's office breathing down my neck, demanding this semester's fees. I never told Dad I quit school and he never asked, until he ran into me at the Livingston Mall, where I was vending tie-dyes and Guatemalan shwag from a pushcart.

HETH GRADUATED FROM junior college with a two-year degree in the behavioral sciences (not sure what he hoped to do with that lucrative puppy) and I was a music school dropout. With no prospects and absolutely no idea what to do next, we both moved back home with Mom. Thankfully, later that summer there was a reprieve from the drudgery of my day job when Mom's therapist Dan awarded both of us "student scholarships" to attend his annual meditation retreat at Gaia House in Devon, England. We'd heard all about retreats from Mom. They could be difficult at times, she said, but the intensive conditions fostered a deeper connection to self-awareness.

We landed at Heathrow and took a number of trains through the hilly English countryside, meeting all kinds of exotic Brits along the way. Some of their accents were so thick we joked, "Excuse me sir, but can you please speak English!" which always elicited a chuckle.

We arrived at the center deliriously tired but enormously happy to be in the nation that spawned so many great bands. I was hopeful the Pet Shop Boys or Frankie Goes to Hollywood might be attending the workshop, but soon discovered it was to be a silent, seven-day retreat, something Dan had neglected to mention. Initially the silence was awkward. Gathering in the dining room for meals, we sounded like a herd of cattle chomping on a haystack. Every chomp and stomach gurgle was amplified in the stillness.

After a few days we got into a rhythm and I noticed we had both begun to savor the silence, especially the freedom from small talk. During one of our first group meditations, with my brain decompressing from the absence of the usual barrage of daily information, I noticed a funny thing. Concentrating on the rise and fall of my breath, I beheld a magnificent, colorful light show unfolding behind my eyelids, centered in my third eye. It lasted until Dan spoke and the sound of his voice sucked me back into the room as if traveling through a cosmic portal. The experience later reframed my tentatively held belief that consciousness continues on after death, only this time the realization presented itself sans hallucinogens and without the accompanying forty-eight-hour hangover.

Meanwhile Heth had noticed a hot babe sitting a few rows in front of him and instantaneously lost interest in all "dimensions" other than hers. Unable to concentrate on their chakras any longer, the two lovebirds broke silence and roamed the ivied hedgerows of West England, canoodling and making plans for when they got back home (she only lived thirty minutes from Livingston, in Manhattan). Back in the States, they dated on and off for a while, but in the end Julie fell for another guy. Up until that point I'd never really seen Heth depressed . . . at least not on account of a broken heart. Even more unusual, for the first time in my life, my big bro looked to me for help and assurance. I surveyed the problem and decided the best course of action would be to get out of Livingston pronto—a change of scenery would do him good.

Just as we got up the nerve to place a deposit on the only thing we could afford (a two-bedroom crack den in Jersey City), we received an unexpected consolation from Heth's failed tryst. Now a realtor, Julie generously offered us the lease to a rocking rent-stabilized apartment only two blocks from Central Park. It turned out to be just what the doctor ordered.

Heth savoring the last few months of being an only child

From left to right: Jed, Flippy, Dad, Heth

ABOVE: In Los Angeles with our parents; BELOW: Heth in his favorite chair

Best buds

Dad at work (right)

ABOVE: One of our first winters in Livingston, New Jersey
BELOW: Mom and Jed with the Dodge Dart

ABOVE: Heth rocking on his first drum set;   BELOW: Jed playing the fluegelhorn

Jed and Dizzy Gillespie,
Washington Square Park,
Greenwich Village

Heth listening to
records on the Pioneer
stereo

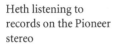

5

Dead-End Jobs and Confused Guitarists

[HETH]

n 1992, Jed and I moved into our rent-stabilized fourth-floor walkup, zip code 10022. The rent was only five hundred bucks a month for an apartment in arguably the most opulent neighborhood on the planet.

Life amongst the nobility was weird. When exiting our building we were regularly cock-blocked by the paparazzi or pushed out of the way by secret service agents protecting people like the Clintons or François Mitterrand, shuffling the elite to and from such shrines as Cipriani and the Grolier Club. There was the ever-present patter of horse-drawn carriages making for the Plaza Hotel or Central Park, both only two blocks away.

Our new digs were squirreled away in the back of the building. We never saw a stitch of direct sunlight and heard barely any street noise except for the distant pounding of garbage trucks around 3 AM. All in all, it was like spelunking in a dark cave in the middle of Manhattan, creating perfect sleeping conditions for us vampires. The apartment seemed to cast a spell on us. As a result, we spent the first few months blissfully sleeping off the wicked hangover of our youth, waking only to catch some afternoon rays up at Sheep

Meadow in Central Park while simultaneously keeping our eyes peeled for potential bandmates.

We were likely the first aspiring musicians to take up residence in the neighborhood in decades. When the Beatles first came to the United States, they holed up at the Delmonico Hotel only a half block up the street, and Led Zeppelin had stayed two blocks north at the Regency Hotel while filming *The Song Remains the Same*. Nowadays though, the area was dead at night, and in the daylight it teemed with impeccably dressed office peeps and eccentric lady millionaires in freakishly large chapeaus, expertly escorted by doormen along the treacherous journey from a Bentley to the front entrance of Caviarteria.

We regularly embarked on skateboard reconnaissance missions, scavenging the Upper East Side for prime furnishings left on the curb and finding chairs, lamps, and even a desk or two to adorn our new place. We had no radio or television and no money for concerts or movies. A big night out for us was a $3.95 soy burger dinner at Dojo on St. Mark's Place and then over to Bleecker and Bowery to catch a few bands at CBGB. Sometimes we even sprung for the $1.25 subway ride home. But mostly we hung around our sparse digs fumbling through the creation of our first songs, a process full of trial and error, but mainly error.

Late at night we'd return to skating the smooth marble of the sprawling office building complexes that littered Sixth Avenue, usually ending up at the Pulitzer Fountain in front of the Plaza Hotel to smoke a cigarette and ruminate. There was hardly a soul in sight, only the whoosh of an occasional taxi and the comings and goings of the usual suspects: high-class hookers buzzing around the Plaza and Essex House and a few homeless people sleeping on concrete benches.

One sweltering summer night, we were cooling off by the fountain when a freaky dreadlocked blond dude skated up to us like we were old friends.

"Hey dudes, I'm Malcolm," he said, staring deeply into our eyes. "I'm a music producer in need of musicians. You guys play . . . right?"

"Yeah, but how did you . . ."

"Listen," he interrupted. "We're going to start a band together to heal the world. Auditions won't be necessary; you're definitely the chosen ones."

"We're the what?" we asked, laughing.

He handed us a pamphlet that read: *Join the 2nd Avenue Martial Arts Studio.* It featured pictures of Steven Tyler and a few guys from Def Leppard all with arms draped across Malcolm's shoulders like they were best buds. Before fading into the Central Park fog, he pointed to the phone number on the pamphlet . . .

"Dudes," he said. "Call me."

FOR OUR FIRST band rehearsal, we found ourselves in windswept John Jay Park, just off the East River, wielding three-foot Chinese swords and learning a martial art called Qigong, similar to Tai Chi. Gusts of dead leaves crackled across the basketball court as Malcolm instructed, "Now try it again, guys, only lean in this time! Hold the sword higher, then exhale as you bring it down."

"What does this have to do with music?" we wondered.

That question always elicited the same cryptic response: "Don't think. Do your job." This tagline was also repeated in his pamphlet.

I was the drummer, having not yet made the jump to guitar. Jed, however, had already effortlessly switched from trumpet to bass, putting to use some of his music school training. Malcolm's hot, dread-headed wife One Love (or One Slave, as we later referred to her) completed the line-up as guitar player and den mother of sorts, cooking us macrobiotic meals, at one point even giving us acupuncture. Looking back now, it was insane for us to let people we barely knew stick needles in us.

"Before we met," Malcolm told us between rigorous daily martial arts workouts, "I knew you two were close by. In fact, I'd been telling One Love my disciples were near. Didn't I, honey?"

"Sure did, hon."

". . . disciples?"

"Yes, we've shared many lives together," he explained. "We were soldiers in Egypt during the time of the Great Pyramids. And guys, check this out, I've decided to train you once again as my bodyguards."

Part of us wanted to believe him; our hunger for rock stardom blinded us and made us ripe for the picking. At Malcolm's urging, we even moved in to his dojo for a spell. He ruthlessly targeted our weaknesses, lecturing us on the things we'd done wrong in our current and past lives and prodding us to turn our backs on friends and family. At times he even blocked outside phone calls. All the while he dangled the carrot of musical fame and fortune, claiming, "Once we finish our demo, I'm going to call in a favor to my old pal Clive Davis"—then the president of Arista Records.

Luckily, cooler heads prevailed. Jed and I were not about to give ourselves over to a Jim Jones type, so after a few weeks of unsuccessful brainwashing, we made a break for it, explaining we had an unavoidable gig with our old band back in Jersey. This way we could remove our instruments from the dojo and get the hell away from this freakazoid before he could use any of his ancient Chinese sword fighting techniques on us.

A couple days after the prison break, Malcolm called; we let it go to voicemail. "Heth, Jed," he whispered creepily, making us strain to hear. "You're throwing your lives away just as you have done many times before. Without my guidance, you will never make anything of yourselves. You have one hour to call me back." *Click.* It appeared there were people in the world desperately in need of privates for their personal armies. We promised each other we'd be more careful next time.

WHEN YOU'RE BROKE, you take whatever job you can get. Jed and I did a stint together as event photographers. One job that sticks out in my mind is the bar mitzvah of the heir to a major fast food fortune at the Pierre Hotel on Fifth Avenue, complete with a disco set-up, scantly clad dancers hanging from cages, smoke machines, a band, a DJ, a carnival, a make-your-own-video booth, magicians, a petting zoo, and so on. When, in keeping with the Dark Continent theme, the bar mitzvah kid made his entrance on the shoulders of four African Americans dressed as Zulu tribesmen, Jed and I took cover by the free sushi bar.

But that was nothing compared to the Sunday our boss sent us out to photograph a mob wedding over on Flatlands Avenue in Brooklyn. We knew we were in way over our heads when several guests referred to us loudly as "longhaired faggots."

"Okay, smile for me," I said undaunted, photographing a young lady who'd been staring at me all evening. With each shot, her short, meat-headed companion became more and more incensed. I wondered what gave until he walked up and point blank asked me if I was trying to fuck his wife. Before I could muster a response, he cold-cocked me. I fell back dazed, blood oozing from a gash above my eye, staining my one and only suit. When I regained my balance and reality came flooding back into focus, I just barely made out Jed sitting on the guy's chest, pummeling the hell out of him. After the maître d' broke it up, we insisted he call the cops even though he warned we'd only be making it worse for ourselves. When the cops finally arrived, they were dead set against crashing the party.

"Go in there and do your fucking jobs!" I demanded.

"Don't tell us what to fucking do," a cop replied, in one of the thickest New York accents I'd ever heard. "Maybe we'll arrest you for disorderly. Would you like that?"

Then I got word that the newlyweds, perched like a king and queen on hideous wicker thrones, were asking to speak to me. I grudgingly agreed, thinking they were going to apologize, or better yet, hand me a hundred-dollar bill for my troubles, but instead they asked me to finish up the shoot.

"Right after you give me the name of the guy who jumped me," I yelled over "Celebration" by Kool & the Gang. Of course, that wasn't going to happen (Mafia code and all), so Jed and I bailed, leaving twenty thousand dollars worth of photography equipment unattended. Before we drove off, we called our boss to tell him to go pick up his shit.

The next week we went looking for new jobs. I learned that it's best to wait until you don't have a black eye before dropping off applications. Nevertheless, we gained employment within walking distance of our apartment, at the Hard Rock Cafe clone Planet Hollywood, where we sold hundreds of t-shirts per shift, each costing three times our hourly wage. It was a gold mine—just not for us. Inevitably my hatred for authority got the best of me, and I was fired. Jed, however, remained on the job and was later promoted to waiter. He was lucky that one of our bosses, Eve, a beautiful goth-obsessed rocker chick from the Chicago suburbs, had an eye for him. (A few years later this same guardian angel became his wife—but we'll get to that a little later.)

Meanwhile, I'd already found my next job by way of a friend who recommended me for a position at Calling All Pets, a pet shop up way up on Eighty-fourth Street and York Avenue. There, I felt exiled to the edge of the universe, indentured to fanatical Upper East Side dog owners, most of whom owned nervous, cupcake-sized pups constantly shivering with inconsolable fear and neuroses. Some customers even wore their canines strapped like helpless newborns to their chests, while others stuck to the local fashion: schlepping them around in baby carriages.

With just five warm bodies in the pet store, my only comic relief came by way of Marco, the delivery guy, a tough barrio kid who was also put in charge of the massive mouse problem in the cellar. Marco developed a ritual of sorts: euthanizing mice with a hammer to the brain before inserting their bloody corpses into the coin return of the corner pay phone. In the summer, he'd sit out front drinking beers, waiting for some poor sucker to come along and put their hand into the slot, looking for change. Then he'd run into the store grinning. The months wore on uneventfully until the day he didn't show up for work. Turns out he'd been having some problems with kids who were harassing him, trying to steal his new coat. One day he snuck his brother's .38 out of the house and the next time those kids jumped him, he shot one in the stomach. Marco spent his seventeenth birthday locked up at Rikers. He'd never meant to actually kill anyone, but since his mom couldn't afford legal counsel or bail, he continued on as guest of the state for years to come.

The place wasn't the same without him, but I hung in for a few more months. Once, when the bell clanged, I emerged from the stockroom to keep an eye on a couple of biker dudes in leather jackets who seemed to be casing the joint. One had long bushy hair and the other was a bleached-blond skinhead, anorexic-thin. Sensing trouble, I cautiously approached, asking if they needed any help. In a cool raspy voice, the blondie said, "I'm looking for a cat toy." Then I realized that he was actually a she, and a pretty cute one at that. I was determined to get to the bottom of this.

"Hey, are you guys in a band?" I asked, my inner rocket scientist kicking in. She mumbled something about the Blackhearts.

Fucking hell! It was Joan Jett with a radically new hairdo. I was so embarrassed that I hadn't recognized one of my all-time heroes up close that after she left the shop, I went into one of my deep funks, wondering how the hell I was ever going to break into the music business if I couldn't even recognize rock royalty when it was asking me for a cat toy.

STILL A LITTLE shell-shocked by our close call with the Cult of Malcolm, Jed and I regrouped with an eye toward forming a new band. Instead of dipping into the vast talent pool of New York City guitarists, we pussed out and called our old pal Steve from Livingston—the cool kid who'd let me use his drum kit many years before. In addition to being one of our best friends and an Ed's room alumnus, the musical prodigy from back in the 'hood brought a great ear to the fold. When he felt like it, he could rip a guitar solo on his Telecaster that would make your balls tingle.

Our new band, Airport Hug, shared a one-room rehearsal space with three other bands on West Twenty-sixth Street and Seventh Avenue, right around the corner from the Fashion Institute of Technology. But whereas clusters of luxury condos currently dot every square block of that area, the neighborhood at that time was desolate, dangerous even in daylight, except on Sundays when vacant parking lots sprouted flea markets like poppies after a rain.

EXITING THE N train, we regularly strolled past freshly assembled Santería shrines flickering in darkened vestibules and flower arrangements piled high on bloodstained sidewalks, commemorating the latest murder. As we passed through the glass entrance gate to the building, we were greeted by a set of overflowing raccoon-resistant garbage cans that hadn't been emptied in eons, their stench permeating the building. Our hearts skipped a beat when mysterious wildlife dove past, leaping from ginormous garbage piles like squirrels rustling through dead leaves in the Jersey woods. The hazardous elevator ride to the ninth floor was punctuated by the ominous clanking of chains as the car swung wildly from side to side. The elevator inspection certificate posted inside was signed M. Mouse, then, underneath, D. Duck and B. Bunny. Destitute musicians regularly made off with the hallway light bulbs, so the trick was to have your keys ready before exiting the elevator, as it was pitch black in the corridor. I won't even mention the bathroom situation except to say we tried not to go except in extreme emergencies, but we preferred to climb out onto the fire escape and whiz into the courtyard.

The main source of the gathering filth was a homeless jazz bassist named Ted who'd taken up residence in the custodial closet at the end of the hallway. Though a semi-cool guy and an incredible bass player, he was a pig. Ironically, he'd been hired to straighten up the place for the never-present landlord, Kenwood Dennard, a legendary drummer who spent most of his time on the road with the likes of Sting, Jaco Pastorius, and the Gil Evans Orchestra. Ted's inability to do his job forced all the bands on the floor to rebel with a half-assed rent strike, which eventually led to his expulsion. But it was too late. A massive infestation of flies and vermin had already made his astonishing pile of refuse their permanent home.

There were probably eight other bands rehearsing on the ninth floor, all with distinctly different vibes. We watched enviously as two of them signed with major record labels—Brit pop shoegazers Mach Five with Island Records, and downtown darlings Jonathan Fire Eater with Geffen Records. Though frustrating, their success kept us well motivated. We had a pretty decent song war going with Fire Eater, for a time. We thought they were dicks and hated their brand of bourgeois trust fund rock, so after listening to them hacking away at one of their pretentious tunes through the thin particleboard ceiling for what seemed like hours, we'd had enough. When they took a break we returned the favor, blasting them with our own twisted interpretation of their song. Take that, suckers! We triumphantly went back to work, until through that same porous ceiling we heard them brilliantly retaliating with a painful rendition of one of our own songs. Touché, gents.

Our songwriting reflected the angst-ridden grunge of the mid-'90s, which was fitting, considering the three of us were stressed out to the max and constantly at each other's throats. Adding to our anxiety was the perpetual challenge of getting Steve to contribute. At rehearsals he'd check his watch more often than a track coach.

Despite Steve's relentless pessimism, Jed and I believed in our latest songs wholeheartedly. Loyal to a fault, and mistakenly under the impression that he was irreplaceable, we let him get away with minimal day-to-day involvement. We did all the promotional mailings, booked all the gigs, arranged all transportation, even roadied his equipment. All he had to do was show up and play.

Steve was an aspiring tennis pro and, much to our dismay, dressed like he'd just stepped off the court. We had a million band meetings about it, yet it remained impossible for him to stop wearing such un-rock'n'roll attire as khakis and pastel-colored polo shirts.

"Dude," we'd chide, "you're not in Color Me Badd!"

Alas, any calculated fashion purchase such as a halfway-cool t-shirt or tight jeans might be interpreted as dedication. Whenever he felt backed against a wall during one of our invariably heated band meetings, he'd nervously practice his backhand, complete with imaginary racket. I don't one-hundred-percent blame the dude, considering it wasn't always easy being cooped up with Jed and me. We were pretty intense when in survival mode, which, back then, was most of the time.

OUR FAVORITE PLACE to play was world-famous CBGB, despite the fact that booking a gig there was always an epic undertaking. The club's phones were either constantly ringing or intentionally off the hook. The best way for local bands to get a show there was to pop over in the flesh on Tuesday or Thursday afternoons to check avails with the talent booker, Louise Staley (with whom Jed and I were both secretly in love). Since CB's had launched the careers of so many of our heroes—Blondie, Television, Patti Smith, the Ramones, and Talking Heads—each visit was akin to a pilgrimage to Mecca. To maintain our composure we'd take a few calming breaths before entering the club; then, grabbing hold of the springy wooden front door, we'd prepare for the initial hit of dirty mop and stale beer. It blew over us like a divine breeze. Once inside, we stood motionless for a minute until our eyes adjusted and the darkness finally revealed the grey-haired owner, Hilly Kristal, unfailingly perched at his desk.

The great thing about playing CB's was it didn't matter if you were an unknown or if you were big-time; every band received the dignity of a stellar light show and, of course, full use of the deafening sound system. Another peculiarity of the club was Hilly's dog, which was more punk than any of us. It roamed freely through the dim shadows, taking shits wherever it pleased, like a canine GG Allin (the downtown shock rocker who often defecated on stage and threw it at the audience). Many were the times unsuspecting rockers left the club wondering how they'd gotten dog shit all over their new Doc Martens.

Airport Hug concluded a deafening nine-song set at CB's one night when, with my ears still ringing and amidst a thick haze of cigarette smoke, perspiration, and twentysomething angst percolating throughout the room, I grabbed this hot babe co-worker of mine and started making out with her.

Like me, Hope was a displaced refugee from New Jersey (Garden State Parkway, Paramus exit 163, to be exact; guess I had to move all the way to the city to fall in love with a Jersey Girl). She was then sharing an apartment on Thompson Street in the West Village with her sister and two cats, Jack and Milo, while holding down several jobs and taking a full course load at the astronomically expensive New York University. We'd met working as waiters at the short-lived Fashion Cafe in the heart of Rockefeller Center during the inexplicable explosion of theme restaurants that plagued New York City in the mid- to late-'90s (Planet Hollywood, Harley Davidson Café, Motown Cafe, All Star Café, Jekyll and Hyde, and Mars 2112). Fashion, co-owned by figureheads Claudia Schiffer, Elle Macpherson, and Naomi Campbell, featured a tacky, museum-like interior with sneeze-guard style glass encasements shielding clothes worn at one time by the likes of Cindy Crawford, Gianni Versace, Elton John, and Madonna. As far as I was concerned, the CBGB make-out session was a sign from the heavens that Hope and I were meant to be. Two kids against the world, love at first kiss in the coolest anti-establishment watering hole in the universe, a union most definitely blessed by the rock'n'roll deities because we've been together ever since, sixteen years and counting.

AROUND THIS TIME, Jed's girlfriend Eve, now acting as band manager, encouraged us to record a demo to submit to major record companies. We agreed that it did seem like the thing to do, so Jed and I pooled our life savings and splurged on a state-of-the-art Tascam eight-track recorder. After negotiating its steep learning curve, we produced a halfway-decent demo and began contacting labels. To weed out the crap, gatekeepers insisted that artists submit through an attorney or high-powered manager, neither of which we had, so we went through the phone book calling up every label in Manhattan, taking turns pretending to be our own band manager. This worked fine to an extent but mostly resulted in a not-so-sweet pile of rejection letters:

> *Dear Airport Hug,*
> *Thank you for your submission, but we are presently not looking for any new artists. We hope you find a home for your music in the near future.*

After numerous demos and subsequent rounds of submissions some labels grew sick of us entirely. One rejection letter began, "Thank you for the millionth opportunity to listen in on your lives." Despite the negative response we remained tenacious, swaying Steve to chance a self-funded CD, each of us committing one-third of the financing. The idea of investing that kind of money pushed him far out of his comfort zone, but after some expert cajoling and serious hand-holding he ultimately agreed. We immediately booked three days' recording time at Lenny Kravitz's Waterfront Studios in Hoboken. Because it was located just outside Manhattan, we could record and mix our four-song EP for only eleven hundred bucks each. Furthermore, Steve lived only five blocks away, which we hoped boded well for his attendance.

The studio was completely analog, the last of a dying breed. Housed in an abandoned pre-war factory, you had to know where to find the inconspicuous front door to gain entry. Once inside, your senses were overwhelmed by an astonishingly luxurious recording facility. It was like the scene from the James Bond movie *The Man with the Golden Gun*, where MI6's high-tech headquarters are located in a half-sunken ship in Hong Kong Harbor.

We did very little overdubbing or editing, tracking most of the record in a "live room" the size of a high school gymnasium. You could have fit a symphony in there—and they often did. There were also twenty vintage amplifiers to choose from, which instantly sent Steve into guitarist heaven, an obvious selling point when we initially toured the facility. Kravitz was an audiophile and Beatles fanatic, having bought the actual *Abbey Road* recording console from EMI Studios. While it looked more like a pizza oven than a classic recording device, its vintage tubes and circuitry lent superior warmth to the recording. By the end of the session we had affectionately named it the Beatle-izer. As in, "Can you Beatle-ize Jed's vocal a little more?" Just touching its hot surface gave us a thrill, knowing the four lads from Liverpool had used it while recording *Sgt. Pepper*.

Charlie, the chain-smoking house engineer, came included in the studio fee. Upon meeting us, he immediately confided that he highly doubted we had what it took to finish and mix in three days, let alone pull off a career in the music business. Continuing to impart confidence, he lamented, "A decent project has never just walked in off the street." We were instantly determined to prove him wrong.

To his credit, despite his reservations, he gave us his all in the studio. He took a few expert hours to mike up my Pearl Export series drums to perfection. On playback, the sound boomed through the massive control room monitors, bouncing off the cushy brown leather sofas. I played the intro to "When the Levee Breaks" from *Zeppelin IV*, just to be sure.

Duh, duh, pop, duh, dee, dee, pop. Duh, duh, pop, duh, dee, dee, pop.

"Yup, frickin' explosive, man," I confirmed, never having heard my drums sound that awesome on tape.

"Bonham only used three microphones on his kit," Charlie said, explaining the classic set-up. "You put one in front of the kick drum and one overhead microphone on each side of the room."

While we were warming up on "Fade," the first song of the session, we were encouraged to see a crowd of studio employees gathering. They liked that we were throwing down old school (i.e., actually playing our instruments as a live band) but more so, were getting off on this scrappy little band that had the balls to take on such a Herculean project on their own dime. After a few hours, even Charlie came around and began rooting for us. It didn't hurt that Eve had greased him with a batch of chocolate chip cookies she'd baked the night before. It was exactly that kind of quick thinking that helped her win the coveted position of band manager.

Except for the occasional emotional flare-up, the recording was going along relatively well, until our third song, "Life's a Photograph," when Steve freaked.

Life's a photograph
I'm not in
Cutting room floor artifact
I'm destined
Someone said I have a dream
Don't waste my time

"You fucking guys keep speeding up. It's off to the races every time."

Jed and I thought it sounded fine, but after a few more takes he had a full-blown meltdown, throwing his guitar and storming out of the session.

"Steve! Dude!" we called after him. "What the fuck, man?"

About eighty-five bucks later he once again graced us with his presence, returning to "give it another go." After hearing the whole blow-up in high Dolby stereo through a flock of hundred-thousand-dollar Sennheiser microphones, Charlie came out from the control room to ask if we'd humor him for a minute.

"I think we should try a click track on this one."

We agreed and he disappeared back into his lair to make the necessary adjustments. Seconds later we heard a cowbell clanging through our headphones. With Charlie at the helm however briefly, Jed and I felt a huge relief. Steve selected the tempo, and away we went.

A few more takes and we nailed it. The metronome had steadied us. In fact, the problem song, "Life's a Photograph," went on to experience a successful run at hundreds of college radio stations and was even played on the nationally syndicated "Rick Dee's Top Forty Countdown," sandwiched between Hootie and the Blowfish and the Counting Crows. Not bad for a cookie-fueled project that had "just walked in off the street."

Amazingly, in the months that followed, record labels such as Columbia and Mercury came by CBGB to check us out. It felt incredibly gratifying to finally have label interest, but the tension in Airport Hug was palpable. Emotions were bubbling over, so much so that we found ourselves fighting over stupid stuff like which song to play for a friggin' sound check. As record companies began to show interest, we had to ask ourselves if Steve was a self-saboteur when, seemingly for no reason at all, he set about killing our hard-won momentum.

"I believe my guitar riffs are more important than any other component of the song," he announced one day after rehearsing "Homegrown."

Homegrown baby
Came from the neighborhood
Homegrown
Loving this feeling
Homegrown baby
Kicking it like we should
In my old neighborhood

"If any one of us ever left the band—and I'm just saying hypothetically—if I leave, I take my guitar riffs with me. Right?"

This theory was far from how the concept of song ownership is commonly understood. Songs don't cease to exist because a partnership has ended; remaining members continue to share royalties with ex–band members. Still, we got the drift. Even more disheartening was the feeling of impending betrayal by an Ed's room alumnus, a guy for whom we would have taken a bullet.

Steve kept yammering on with his frustrating, untenable argument. His points seemed all the more asinine considering our present situation. We were fighting over possible future income, sweating our nuts off in an unventilated, crap-hole rehearsal room in one of the most cracked-out neighborhoods of the city. So finally, to settle the matter, Jed and I had an attorney draw up a contract stating categorically that all songs were equally owned. The attorney predicted it would make Steve either "shit or get off the pot." He was right: Steve most definitely took a shit. He signed the contract, but at the very next rehearsal he showed up cocked and ready to blow.

"I have something to tell you guys." Long, dramatic pause . . . "I'm quitting the band."

"What? Why? What about the Mercury Lounge gig?"

"Nope," he said sneering. "Can't do it."

Jed said, "In that case, I need some fucking air. When I come back you better have all your shit the fuck out of our room."

We never heard from our "brother" again.

After he quit, we had two weeks to draft a replacement guitarist for a record label showcase at the Mercury Lounge. In desperation we placed an ad in the back of the *Village Voice* and hoped for the best. To our surprise, calls poured in. We immediately scheduled auditions, feeling optimistic.

Our first applicant arrived with four humongous Marshall stack amplifiers, defying our directive to use our amps, already set up in the room. It took him and a roadie three elevator trips before the whole deal was set up. He must have gotten confused and thought we were playing a show over at Madison Square Garden instead of our nine-by-ten rehearsal room. He assured us it would be worth the wait because we "need not look no further."

"Okay, lets start with 'So Easy,'" I said. "One, two, three, four!"

"Hold on, hold on," he said, taking off his shirt to expose his tattoos and nipple piercings.

"Okay, ready now?"

"Yeah," he said, "let's do it," and let go with the loudest set of power chords we'd ever heard. I think we're still deaf from it, every chord drilling into our ear canals like a jackhammer. *GAGAAAAAAHHH! GAGAAAAAAHHH! GAGAAAAAAHHH! GAGAAAAAAHH-HEEEEEEOOOOSSSSSHHHZZZZZ!*

We felt like the guy in the classic Maxell tape ad who gets his hair blown back by the raging wall of sound blasting from his stereo.

"Okay! Thanks!" we yelled, trying to get his attention over the shrill feedback. "Thanks for coming down, man. We'll let you know."

He took an inordinate amount of time packing up his gear. When he finally exited the room, he glared at the next candidate and informed us he "wasn't into playing pussy music anyways."

Twenty auditions later, the ad had been a complete bust. For one reason or another, nobody had really clicked. Then, in a stroke of amazing luck, a friend of ours who played with Widespread Panic put us in touch with a former bandmate. By this time, we'd learned to feel out prospective guitarists before inviting them down to West 26th. Drake sounded more than professional over the phone, and as expected, he aced the audition, effortlessly playing our songs better than Steve ever had.

"No offense," Drake said, "but the guitarist on your last CD sounded a bit outdated. He was kind of a hack."

We liked him instantly.

With a new guitarist in the band, we experienced a surge of creativity, not only rocking the fuck out of the Mercury Lounge but getting down to work on a brand new CD as well.

Even though Steve bailed on performing that last show, he did manage to make it to the club on time, even forking over the ten bucks to stalk our new guitarist.

DRAKE HAD PRODUCED a few CDs in his day. With high hopes, we handed over the production reins, giving him just two directives: get us in and out of Baby Monster Studios on budget, and with a kick-ass CD. By this time, Waterfront Studios had been shut down to make way for waterfront condos. Sadly, this meant no Beatle-izer for our vocal tracks, but the house engineer fortuitously appointed to our session was a guy named Jamie Candiloro. Together we bonded over a shared musical vision. Throughout the next several years, Jamie came to have a dramatic and lasting effect on our career, ultimately producing all our Heth and Jed CDs.

The recording process started off with us banging out keeper tracks left and right. We had a great head of steam going until the Draker started showing up in altered states. When it was time for him to record his guitar parts, he'd procrastinate or go missing altogether. Though he could still muster a twang here and there, there was no creative fire behind his playing. Never mind Elvis leaving the building, Drake had left the planet.

"Drake dude, how can we help you?" we begged, each of us with four thousand dollars in credit card debt riding on the finished product.

He responded with some kind of gibberish, agonizing over his "inner child" and accusing us of "not understanding how hard it is to play guitar." We were living a bad movie plot. In an effort to take back control and salvage what we could, we had no choice but to eject him from the control room. With the clock ticking, we attempted to play Drake's parts ourselves while he sat in the lobby making nice with the studio's tropical fish. Ultimately we had to can him and go even deeper into debt hiring replacements to finish up the remaining guitar tracks. Once the recording was complete, we printed a thousand CDs, but without a guitarist, label interest dissipated and the disc never saw the light of day.

I am happy to report that Drake did eventually regain his senses and become coherent enough to email us cryptic death threats in the form of song lyrics, liberally quoting verses from "Instant Karma" and the always snappy "Happiness Is a Warm Gun." The Drakester always was a huge Beatles fan.

His meltdown signified the end of a stressful era. Broke and burned out, Jed and I had serious questions about ourselves. Why were we so musically codependent? And why did our father keep manifesting in the form of guitarists? With our creative energy waning and uncertain how to proceed, we made the difficult choice to pull the plug on the band. It was time for some much needed perspective.

6

Communication Breakdown

[JED]

The love between Eve and me was strong and real, but there were a number of outside forces working against us, which is probably why it took me eight years to finally pop the question. For one thing, I was seven inches shorter than she was, and that's when she was in flats. Though the height difference was inconsequential in our eyes, we had an uncanny knack for catching shit wherever we went, especially on the streets of Manhattan, where apparently I was invisible. We never got a break from dudes whistling, catcalling, and throwing cheesy lines at her left and right: "Hey baby, lose that zero and get with a hero!" Or, "You may be tall, but we're all the same size when we're horizontal." Guys her height often accosted me, complaining I'd unfairly taken one of their "sisters" off the market.

Another problem was the inordinate number of stalkers she attracted. One creepy dude made it his mission in life to trail her around the city for months at a time. It was nerve-racking for the both of us.

"Owww, what the hell?" I whined, as Eve pulled me off the N train by my elbow. "Why are we getting off here?"

"That's him … my stalker," she whispered, sheepishly half-pointing in the direction of a tall, Middle Eastern–looking guy with a long black beard.

"What? Why didn't you fucking tell me while we were in the train?"

"Because of your temper, dude!"

Since the train was pulling out all I could do was smash the door with my fists, yelling, "You're fucking dead, bitch!"

Yet Eve's six-foot-three statuesque beauty could also work in our favor, like the time I made the awesome discovery that if she picked up our BurritoVille order, our white bean chicken chili burritos would be on the house.

I'd have traveled to the edge of the world for my bride, but nevertheless something always went down when we visited that hotbed of stress known as her mom's house, just outside Chi-town. During one visit, Eve's older sister Karen overheard me fondly recalling the time I chucked one of those pastel desk-chair combos at my twelfth-grade teacher, Mrs. Buchwald, after she spontaneously announced in front of the class, "Mr. Weinstein, you are ugly and your clothes are gross and inappropriate." Karen put two and five together and miraculously came up with the harebrained idea that I was beating Eve. As in the classic game of "telephone," the information rapidly mutated as it passed from person to person, and Eve's mom hurried her into the kitchen for interrogation. I could hear the subsequent muffled drama unfolding down the hallway, Evie going to bat for me, arguing that I was in fact an upstanding dude.

The family drama further intensified when, by virtue of Eve's German ancestry and my being a Jew-bag, both our dads declined their wedding invitations. Sad—with so much in common, the two would have gotten on famously. The few times Pop did meet Eve, he left a lasting impression. Like the time he took us out for Chinese food, only to spoil the gesture by slamming her with cheesy Nazi references like "Achtung!" accompanied by the ever-popular "Heil Hitler" salute. Cutting dinner short, I burst out, "Dad, if you ever make another racist comment to my girlfriend, you won't be eating solid food for three months." In my anger, I had turned into him. I didn't know which horrified me more—his newly acquired Tourette syndrome or my own volatile behavior—and I profusely apologized to Evie on both our behalves. Eve's dad was less overt, paying little attention to us. After all our years of dating, he still believed his daughter was marrying some guy named Jet.

Heth and Hope (who happens to be Asian) didn't fare much better with Pops. After graciously inviting them up to his house for Passover dinner, he called back half an hour later. "Listen, ummm . . . sorry, but we've decided no goyim at the table," he said, using a Yiddish phrase meaning non-Jews. When close family friends came from California to visit him and Eleanor, Dad once again pulled the old switcheroo, inviting me and Heth and our girlfriends out to dinner with them, only to cancel at the last minute, explaining that the plans had fallen through. Disappointed, I did what I usually do on a night off: picked up some primo Chinese takeout from my favorite local spot, Congee Village on Allen Street. While paying, I happened to glance into the bamboo forest-themed dinning room, only to see Dad and Eleanor hosting the canceled dinner party. What the fuck? I contemplated pouring a pot of hot tea on his lap. Instead I swallowed my rage, grabbed my pork lo mein, and steamrolled my way home to Clinton Street, shoulder slamming some unsuspecting hipster exiting the dive bar Welcome to the Johnsons. "Make a fucking move, bitch," I dared him.

Shortly after that, it dawned on me that I'd felt like a lifelong uninvited guest in Dad's world. In an effort to iron things out, I got up the nerve to call him.

"Dad, I saw you at Congee Village."

Crickets.

"You said dinner was canceled, but there you all were, stuffing your faces."

"Look, son, I can't help it if you get hurt by the things you think I do."

"I don't understand how you can lie directly to my face and . . ."

Dad interrupted, "Bottom line is you must obey me no matter how crazy you think I am, or you stand to lose an inheritance of over a million dollars."

Not again! Over the years he'd impetuously added and removed us from his will so many times, it had practically become a time-honored Weinstein family tradition. Any effrontery could be grounds for dismissal.

I let him have it.

"You know what, Dad? Why don't you take your fucking money and *shove it up your ass?*"

After a long, uncomfortable pause he came clean, soberly admitting, "Eleanor hates you and Heth, and there's nothing I can do about it. If I invite you to a family dinner, she'll leave me, and I'm not about to let that happen. I'm sorry son, but that's just the way it is."

Following this blowout, Heth and I saw Dad one more time. Mostly we discussed safe topics like the weather and the art exhibit he'd just seen. Strangely, he wouldn't make eye contact and when it was our turn to speak he'd gaze at the ceiling, whistling. After that, we fell out of touch. Months went by, then years. Though he lived in New Jersey, I'd occasionally spy him plodding the streets of my Lower East Side neighborhood, his own childhood stomping ground, haunting me like an ex-girlfriend. With each encounter, I was increasingly startled by his deteriorating appearance, his sad eyes now sunken and his face pudgy and haggard with age. Once, I noticed him waiting for the F train at the Delancey Street subway station. He was gorging himself on his favorite sweets, chocolate almond bark from Economy Candy. I guess he didn't recognize me, and when the train pulled in he walked by as if I were invisible. Though the rift between us was deep, my mind still flooded with happy childhood memories—his contagious laugh, flute lessons in his study, the Wo Hop fireworks adventures, and how, as tykes, he picked us up, tickling us with kisses on our tiny bellies. I boarded the same car and secretly rode alongside him with tears in my eyes, paralyzed in my stupid pain, conflicted and unable to reach out. At the very least, I wanted to be in his presence one more time.

MEANWHILE, DESPITE OUR years of therapy, Heth and I became experts at shutting each other out. Our brotherly rift lasted almost two years. We had perfected the art of carrying early childhood dysfunction around with us, unintentionally depositing large doses into the heart of the band until its final collapse, and neither of us could back down from a juicy fight. The famously feuding brothers from the band Oasis had nothing on us.

During that time I auditioned for a bunch of lame bands and studied digital audio engineering, while Heth worked as drummer for hire, mostly speed drumming with a pop-punk band called Dirt Bike Annie. Heth accompanied Dirt Bike on frequent Midwest tours, primarily playing Veterans of Foreign War halls, community centers, game rooms, and even the occasional basement.

"So dudes . . . we don't have a place to crash tonight . . ." they often announced from the stage. "Anybody wanna take home a slightly used band?"

When the gang pulled into Columbus for a gig at an off-campus house, Heth noticed an inordinate number of swastikas in the vicinity. Some were tattooed on the arms of their hosts, others hovered overhead, draped across the ceiling in the form of large Third Reich flags. He privately voiced his reservations to his bandmates, whispering, "Dudes, do me a favor and *do not*—I repeat, please *do not*—let anyone know I am Jewish."

Confident they had his back, he went for a walk, finding a little mom-and-pop liquor store where he immediately scored a six-pack of the first thing he saw. When he returned from the beer run, it was apparent the cat's ethnicity was out of the bag.

"Listen man, we ain't got nothing against you . . . but seriously, why did you guys kill Christ?"

Another guy added, only half-jokingly, "We might have to lynch us a Jeeeew before the night is threeeew."

"Ha ha. Real funny, guys," Heth responded, feeling like a gay kid outed at a Young Presbyterians' meeting. Just as the pre-show tension was becoming too much to bear, the head Nazi noticed what Heth was drinking: a can of the celebrated local suds. He had unknowingly picked up the holiest of holy indigenous beer, the only strain that garnered respect from the Nazi punk chapter of Columbus, Ohio. After receiving all kinds of accolades and pats on the back for his mystical selection, they assured him, "C'mon dude, we could never lynch anyone with such good taste."

"READY FOR BED, Mr. Weinstein?"

"Sure am babe, er, I mean, Mrs. Weinstein," I replied to my bride of only a few hours. Maybe it was the never-ending supply of Piper-Heidsieck talking, but Eve kept calling me Mr. Weinstein, as if we'd both undergone the marital name change.

Our wedding ceremony took place amid the peaceful turquoise waves at the farthest tip of a long wooden dock at Compass Point in Nassau, Bahamas. Our moms attended the intimate affair, as did Heth and Hope. Heth had graciously consented to be best man even though by this time the emotional tumor formed during the band's break-up had metastasized. In other words, we hated the fuck out of each other. For almost a year prior to the nuptials, we'd scarcely hung out at all except at the occasional holiday dinner, over a platter of Mom's mouthwatering, peace-engendering brisket and potatoes.

No matter, Evie and I were thrilled to have family along, especially considering that in a fit of excitement we'd nearly eloped a month earlier. But our moms would have none of that. No problemo: Compass Point was fully equipped for last-minute weddings, with everything kept low-key—especially the killer kind bud the cabana boys sold us. Our accommodations were elevated huts teetering above the ocean on stilts, which allowed for instant decompression, everyone enjoying the soothing sound of the sea lapping underneath— and all those negative ions working their magic. On our special day, Eve wore a sexy white halter dress while Heth and I donned rad surf trunks with flames shooting up the sides. With a red sunset blazing overhead we said our *I dos*, then partied for a week straight.

The resort's close proximity to the famous Compass Point recording studio didn't mean that much to Eve, but for me it was like sleeping a hundred feet from the Sistine Chapel. In an effort to bury the hatchet with big broski, I'd been trying to hook up a surprise tour of the historic facility, but the studio was closed to the public, and it seemed nearly impossible. So I enlisted my secret weapon, sending my charming bride to lay it on thick with the concierge. Half an hour later she returned with a confirmed appointment. They'd graciously fit us in just behind the Backstreet Boys' exit and prior to U2's arrival. But unfortunately, instead of relishing the experience, with each platinum album we encountered—Iron Maiden's *Piece of Mind*, the Stones' *Emotional Rescue*, and AC/DC's *Back in Black*, just to name a few—Heth and I felt more and more alienated, trapped in some giant rock'n'roll cock tease. The torture continued as we happened upon the remnants of the past week's recording session. The names of various Backstreet Boys were still inscribed on the corresponding faders of the mixing console: *Track 28: Nick intro oohs. Track 34: AJ 2nd chorus harmony*, et cetera. We fucking hated their music but coveted their success, and of course their sweet record deal.

Upon our return: "How was the studio?"

"Fucking great, ladies!" we replied in unison, each ordering a double Jim Beam on the rocks.

But against all odds, time spent together on the island yielded a sort of détente between us. With the sun and surf softening our brotherly feud, Heth and I began to let go of lingering grudges, no longer blaming each other for Airport Hug's demise. Heth came clean, admitting that it was difficult for him to have Eve as both band manger and sister-in-law, and apologized for any transgressions. In return, I apologized for shutting him out.

Over the next year and a half, we grew closer. If we didn't run into each other over at Mom's, we'd make sure to speak on the phone, bonding over shared interests like a new song one of us was writing or some happening new band. Slowly our desire to perform together was reignited. We even went out for two-dollar beers at the Subway Inn, the dive bar across the street from Bloomingdales. That's when Heth dropped it on me, recounting his tale of cosmic epiphany, explaining how after the Dirt Bike Annie tour, he'd been job-hunting when an unscheduled stop at a neighborhood church yielded an unexpected spiritual recharge. In mid-prayer, his financial panic had subsided as he felt the faint vibration of a passing subway train rumbling beneath the wooden floor. A firm believer in synchronicity, Heth read it as a sign from above, beseeching him to *go forth, young man, and take thy music to the subway.* Amen, brothers and sisters!

I have to admit that I was way inspired, though I still had my misgivings. On the subway ride home, I could barely sit still as I imagined how this would play out: Could Heth's newly acquired guitar skills cut it live? Would I have the guts to play in the streets? I decided I didn't care, that it was worth the gamble. But I had to figure a way to break it to Eve since she and Heth still had unresolved issues from the Airport days. I was careful to broach the subject over a bottle of her favorite vino.

"Wanna hear something cool, hon? Heth's been busking around the train stations and doing pretty well at it."

She couldn't have cared less, until she heard the part about me potentially joining him. Then her ears perked up, big time.

"What do you mean, joining him?"

"You know, like starting a band again," I answered shyly. "But this time we're going to do it way differently."

"Jed, you must be crazy. Heth treats you like total shit, and I'm positive that will never change. You're making a huge mistake."

By now, Eve's executive assistant career had grown, and so had her bank account. Her latest job had her assisting three millionaires who ran an international stock-trading company. These dudes were classic CEO types: pop-collared, Rolex-sporting, thoroughly douchetastic, cigar-chomping assholes, arrogant and entitled to the max. They would do anything to gain the upper hand, even steal another man's wife. As they showered her with the finest jewelry and rounds of stock options, the prospect of being married to a budding street musician, as opposed to the previously envisioned rock star, must have been hard for her to take. I felt helpless as we drifted further and further apart.

After a long day at work she'd typically barrel into our apartment, excited to relay endless stories in praise of some billion-dollar deal "her guys" had just wrapped. In a last-ditch effort to reassert my status as one of "her guys," I picked up a couple of *Quark* and *Photoshop for Dummies* books, and set about painstakingly teaching myself graphic design. As it turned out, I took to it relatively quickly, and it wasn't long before I was making serious bank. Eventually I had enough clients that I was turning work down.

Most of my business came from the recession-proof pharmaceutical advertising industry, making ads for medications whose names I couldn't pronounce if my life depended on it. But I also found work in the publishing industry, highlights of which included a week of endlessly re-touching Paulie Walnuts's face for a *Sopranos* calendar and a boner-inducing book of the complete artwork of the Kama Sutra, where I encountered more genitalia than a Times Square whore. My success barely registered with my new bride, but it did impress fellow designers. Never was this more apparent than the day one of my colleagues asked me how much I had left to pay on my student loans.

"I didn't go to school," I confessed, to the consternation of the recent graduate. Apparently the poor kid owed like seventy grand—surely indentured for life.

"Then how did you learn graphics?"

"Bought some books at Borders."

I didn't mean to blow this dude's mind, but I was proud of teaching myself a trade, especially one that years later would be the perfect complement to running a band.

Sadly, I hadn't noticed any books at the store called *Fixing Your Irreparably Fucked Marriage for Dummies.*

"Honey? I keep having the weirdest dream," I confided, as Eve applied her Smoky Lash mascara, readying herself for another late-night business meeting.

"Really, babe?"

"Yeah. Well . . . we're walking down the street somewhere in the Village, surrounded by a sea of people. Our hands become unlocked and we start drifting away. I'm in a panic trying to get back to you, but no matter what I do we drift farther and farther away until I lose you in the crowd. The worst part is you don't seem to care. Actually, you seem relieved."

Her face turned the whitest shade of pale, and she touched the wall for balance. "It's just a dream, baby," she managed, but my subconscious was hip to the writing on the wall.

The next day, I was in mid-deposit at the Citibank on Fifty-fifth Street and Broadway when it all got to be a little too much for my psyche.

"Hi, yes, I'd like to close my account."

"Well, sir, we sure are sorry to see you go. Reason for closing the account?"

"That would be: None of your business."

"Well, I have to write down some kind of reason."

"The reason is: Give me my fucking money!"

The potent combo of snotty bank employees and fears that Eve was having an affair sent me through the roof. I threw a pen at the teller and stormed out, kicking the glass door as I exited. I must have kicked it pretty good, because it shattered into a million goddamn pieces. I surveyed the pile of glass covering my feet and started trembling. When I saw the crowd of midday luncheoners glaring at me I took off, hauling ass all the way to Seventh Avenue in five seconds flat. Right around Carnegie Hall it hit me. *It's a bank, man! They know exactly who the fuck you are!* So I jogged back to turn myself in, briefly stopping to call Eve with a little heads up.

Trying to catch my breath I said, "Hon, I just freaked out in Citibank because they were rude assholes. I threw a pen at the teller and kicked a glass door so hard it shattered. So I think I'm about to go to jail."

"Okay, babe. Keep me posted," she said, hurrying me off the phone.

"Wait! What do you mean, 'Keep you posted'?"

"Well, what do you need from me?"

"What do I need? I need you to give a shit!"

When I returned, the cops were already investigating. I walked straight up to them and confessed.

"Hey, I'm the guy who broke the door."

At first they didn't believe me, but the bank manager confirmed. They cuffed me and sat me down in the manager's office for what seemed like way too long for anything good to be happening. I sat there trying to get my head around the concept of going to jail when the arresting cop approached me.

"If I were you," he said, uncuffing me, "I'd play the lottery, because this is definitely your lucky day. The bank doesn't want to press charges. Now get the hell outta here and do your banking at a different branch for a while."

I'm fairly certain Eve's fat six-figure bank account saved my ass, although nothing could do the same for our marriage. A year and a half in, and Eve and I were toast.

7

Paid to Practice

[HETH]

Jed and I were contemplating the depressing state of our stalled music careers over a spicy plate of aloo gobi and a couple of pints of Kingfisher at Panna II—hands down *the* best Indian restaurant in all of Manhattan; so good, their colossal cockroach infestation was excusable. In the dinning room, beneath dangling reams of flickering chili pepper Christmas lights, we acknowledged that we'd wasted years waiting for the right guitarist to materialize. We also concluded we'd spent far too long on the rehearsal room hamster wheel, over-preparing for unprofitable tours that, in the end, barely broke even after the cost of van rental and gasoline.

We commiserated about being trapped in our practice space, essentially an unventilated, four-hundred-dollar-a-month Petri dish, the air eternally fouled by high levels of methane gas and perspiration from the rotating roster of bands rocking out 24/7. The closest we ever came to "real performance conditions" there was when we dimmed the lights or lit a few candles, then ripped through a tight set pretending we were on the main stage at Lollapalooza, sandwiched somewhere between the Red Hot Chili Peppers and Soundgarden. *We love you Cleveland! Thank you! Good night!* Afterwards, we proudly declared to an audience of no one but ourselves—except for a family of rodents living under the drum riser—"Holy shit man, we fucking killed it!"

By the time the samosas hit the table, the conversation had become a lamentation over the death of Manhattan nightlife and the recent surge in high-end real estate that had shut down all our favorite clubs. The intrepid community of artists, immigrants, junkies, and mom-and-pop stores responsible for reviving the long forgotten, hard-partying hoods like the East Village, Alphabet City, and the Lower East Side were being driven out, replaced by an unprecedented invasion of generic chain stores, banks, and whatever they call yuppies nowadays. It was like the circus had left town.

Luckily Jed's graphics job supplied him with enough cheddar to barely hang on to his Lower East Side bachelor pad studio apartment at an overpriced $1,250 a month. And I still had my midtown, rent-stabilized apartment, though I felt like the last remnant of a dead art scene—and let's face it: My age clock was ticking as well. If I wasn't careful, my musical dreams would slip away forever, potentially leaving me trapped in a soul-crushing 9-to-5.

"Listen man," I said, finishing off the last of my beer, smacking the bottle down on an overfed cockroach. "So far, playing in the subway has saved me from losing my apartment, Hope, and my cats. It's been amazing, but I don't think the cops are going to tolerate a loud rock duo down there. I think our ticket is probably more in the midtown area—somewhere around my neighborhood, possibly."

Jed paused, and then was like, "You mean playing on the actual streets?"

"Yeah, dude. Think of it: the first band to rock Fifth Avenue!"

"Hmm . . . that could work. I'm not saying it'll be easy, but I bet if we go out there every day, something will happen for us. I'm totally in, bro!"

But first, we needed help designing a new and improved band manifesto or we'd be doomed to a repeat performance of Airport

Hug, a leaderless band more devoted to quarrelling than rocking. Not sure how to proceed, we warily ventured into a couple of intense joint therapy sessions with our old meditation teacher, Dan. It was like marriage counseling, only for stubborn dipshits who wanted to rock. Dan employed a highly effective tool for reestablishing communication between warring factions. It simply entailed meditating until the energy of the room became balanced. Then, with eyes still closed, we took turns airing dirty laundry, each of us listening to the other's grievances without interrupting. Of course, that was the hardest part.

I guess you could say we *hugged it out, bitches*, emerging from "couples therapy" as if exiting a Native American sweat lodge, both a little more fine-tuned to each other's needs.

CLEANSED OF SIN, our spirits were high, our souls more than intact. We were pumped, replenished and ready to take our music to the streets.

[Cue theme to *Star Wars*.]

On a sunny Wednesday afternoon in April 2003, we lugged a couple hundred pounds of battery-operated music equipment over to the corner of Fifty-eighth Street and Fifth Avenue to play our inaugural busking show. We carried two amplifiers, one acoustic guitar, one electric bass guitar, two microphone stands, two XLR microphone cables, a dozen quarter-inch cables, a couple of tuners, and a diarrhea-inducing number of butterflies in our stomachs. Hoping to benefit from home court advantage, we set up directly across the street from the Plaza Hotel, essentially converting our late night hang spot into our daytime office, which seemed more than logical, considering the area was a ready-made amphitheater complete with a long set of stairs facing Fifth Avenue. People from surrounding buildings often gathered there to chill with a cig or to eat lunch, while tourists took a breather from massive FAO Schwarz shopping sprees. We hoped if all went well they'd take the hint and use the steps as front row seats.

We assembled our gear, flanked on the right by a protective United States Postal Service mailbox and on the left by one of the ever-present hot dog vendors. Through the noxious plumes of smoke wafting up from the seared pushcart mystery meat, I saw Jed flash me a reassuring smile.

"You ready?"

"Yup," I managed, trying not to focus on all that was riding on our little plan. With little to no clue what to do next, we intuitively modeled ourselves after some of the only other bands we'd ever seen rocking the avenues: the Peruvian pan flute bands that often played on 45th and Broadway in front of the Marriot Hotel. For years we'd witnessed local bands Agua Clara and Grupo Wayno pumping their brand of uplifting, life-affirming world music onto Big Apple sidewalks (we'd also caught the part about them selling a hundred CDs an hour). We used their staging as a blueprint, standing with our backs to the avenue, our guitar case conspicuously front and center to catch tips, and our amplifiers facing the surging mass of pedestrians.

Life slowed down around us and adrenaline took over as we took our positions. Each particle of the atmosphere seemed charged with electricity and anticipation. Away we went . . . and man, did we sound like dog shit. We were plagued with technical issues from note one. For one thing, my guitar strap kept unlocking, causing the instrument to crash onto the concrete occasionally, or worse, onto my toes. Having hardly ever played live, I didn't yet know there was a handy little remedy called strap locks. Our dodgy cables kept buzzing and humming, interrupting our show with sporadic bouts of deafening feedback that made poor old ladies plug their ears as they passed. And my inability to play without my eyes glued to the fret board was debilitating. When someone snuck up and yelled, "You rock!" it startled me to the point I lurched backward into oncoming traffic. Not exactly the auspicious beginning I'd hoped for.

Folks had no idea what to make of us. I'm sure we came off as exactly what we were: two naive suburban kids with guitars strapped to their chests, shyly honking out unrecognizable rock tunes, out of step with the indifferent hip hop/boy band culture of the moment. We felt like we'd crashed someone else's party. No, more like we were zombies crawling into the sunlight after an eternity in purgatory. Either way, the plan was to stay the course, come what may. If people didn't get our peculiar brand of rock'n'roll, we were going to force it down their throats until they did.

About an hour in, we seemed to be warming up. Just as we locked into our first solid groove, some geezer wearing a pair of Coke-bottle glasses and 1950s-style slacks pulled up to his nipples threw our first duo-dollar into the guitar case, and man did that feel good. That's when some cute girls sidled up, asking to take a picture with us. They threw a fiver in the case and jumped between us, putting their arms around our shoulders while their friend beckoned, "Saaaay *queso!*" Before leaving, they gave us the oh-so-continental double cheek kiss. *Ooh-la-la!*

Holy crap, I thought to myself, *this is pretty fucking awesome!*

As the day unfolded, we worked on strengthening our stage legs but kept getting bitch-slapped into submission by the ever-present Fifth Avenue wind tunnel, an unending breeze shooting in off the park and picking up speed as it filtered through the skyscrapers. The persistent gusts wreaked havoc on us, alternating between blowing over our microphone stands and sending us wading into perilous Fifth Avenue traffic to chase down hard-earned dead presidents. One thing had become clear to us: you can train unendingly in musical boot camp, but there's no substitute for live ammo flying overhead.

There was also the complication of our inner suburban child-selves colliding with the reality of gritty New York street life. This became especially apparent when an imposing, homeless-looking guy wearing an orange and white hospital registration bracelet begged us to let him give a "shout-out to the world." Based on his appearance, we were fearful he might beat the shit out of us or maybe grab a handful of our cash if we balked, so under fear of repercussions, we agreed.

"Take it away, man."

"Thanks, rocker dude," he said. Then, spitting all over my microphone: "Hey people, this is what New York is all about! I'm sober five days and you know what? This is life right here, what these two boys are doing with their music. God bless New York! I'm outty."

He threw a Hefty bag of recyclables over his shoulder, tossed a granola bar in our case, and gave us each a resounding fist pound. A foreign couple, dressed in bright, happy European colors, golf-clapped for him, inciting a gaggle of well-dressed women in business suits to request "Jeremy." Though it was only 11 AM, they'd already indulged in something of a liquid lunch.

"C'mon darlings," they encouraged. "Here's twenty-five bucks."

"Deal!" Jed quickly responded.

We instantly violated our no-cover-tunes rule long enough to launch into one helluva horrifying rendition of Pearl Jam's classic. I even broke out my lame Eddie Vedder impersonation for the occasion: "Je–re-mays spo-kane, spo-kane ha-henn, Je–re-mays spo-kane, spo-kane ha-henn . . ."

It had been a long day. We packed up our gear and walked our sunburned asses the three short blocks back to my apartment. I'd just played more in a single afternoon than I had all month. With little in the way of protective calluses, my virgin fingers were blistered and achy from pressing the sharp steel guitar strings. I also had a nasty cramp in my left shoulder where the strap had dug in.

There had been a lot of trial and error out there and we'd definitely learned a thing or two regarding rocking in the streets. As we marched along, I vividly remembered the face of each person who had generously dropped something into our case, as if it was occurring again, right in that miraculous moment. Once home, we dumped the cash out on the floor, looked at each other, and started laughing. We'd just been paid a couple hundred bucks to practice.

8

Urban Frankenstein

[JED]

We became musical Bedouins, settling into a nomadic lifestyle of roving the metropolis with instruments in tow, in search of our next sonic oasis. We called it guerilla busking: show up, plug in, rock out. Then, wash, dry, and repeat. Years of skateboarding Manhattan's pockmarked streets put us at a slight advantage, since we already viewed public spaces far differently from the way ordinary civilians did. It turned out that busking was only a minute chromosomal mutation away from skating. Each sterile grey building embankment that had previously beckoned our Tony Alva skate decks was now a potential concert hall, another stop on our balls-to-the-wall, nonstop tour of Manhattan.

In an effort to add quality real estate to our ever-expanding portfolio of workable performance locations, we investigated prospective venues using a simple litmus test: we'd rock said coordinates until kicked out, ticketed, or both. The process hipped us to the fact that buskers are perilously positioned on the front lines of the battle to preserve the First Amendment. In the years since we'd scored our fake IDs in Times Square, the city had suffered increasingly from creeping authoritarianism. As the junkies and prostitutes were forced out, it became safer to walk the streets, but it also meant that artists and street performers like us were subject to unprecedented levels of scrutiny and harassment. With little by way of induction ceremony, we unintentionally assumed the role of free speech advocates. We'd either rise to the occasion, flipping a primal middle finger to all forms of oppression, or end up crushed by the machine—which nearly occurred when we naively set up shop on the corner of Broadway and Forty-ninth Street during the Republican National Convention of 2004.

Unaware that Times Square was under unofficial martial law lockdown, we kicked off our show with a sincerely patriotic rendition of "The Star-Spangled Banner," but a wandering group of Republican conventioneers, dressed in American flag shirts, took exception to our interpretation and began heckling us.

"Son, if you continue to mock my country's anthem, I will cut you down where you stand."

"Okay, sir," we responded, "whatever you say!"

Then, as if on cue, the cavalry arrived in the form of a group of anarchists, armed with cameras, faces hidden behind black bandanas and shades.

"They have the right to perform here," they protested. "A little something called free speech. Ever heard of it?"

And just like that, we were caught in the middle of a dick-swinging constitutional debate. Like sharks to a bucket of chum, all the commotion stirred up a nearby pack of riot police. These dudes came heavy, decked out in full body armor, sporting M5s and just itching for something to do.

"What are you two doing?"

"Jamming," I screamed over Heth's screeching guitar.

"I can see that. I'll ask you again. Why are you here?"

"We're here to rock. This is, like . . . our job, man."

Probably hoping to find an incendiary device or a shipment of pirated uranium, they poked through our belongings with the butts of their machine guns. By now we'd heard reports that Mayor Bloomberg was capturing RNC protesters with nets and warehousing them on the piers—some seriously scary shit. Though we knew our rights, we treaded carefully, expressing our unwillingness to be searched but not reacting physically when they kept on digging until the head goon called them off, evidently to save the city from more pressing hazards, or else to save themselves from embarrassment.

Even when the Republican National Convention wasn't in town, entanglements with police were all too commonplace. Their main beef was our flagrant criminal use of amplification. But since strumming acoustically on the deafening streets was like pissing in the rain, we had no alternative but to plug in to be heard. Some cops were cool about it and let us off with a warning, but others handed out ticket after ticket, as if satisfying a personal vendetta. *Thank you, sir! May I have another?*

"Do you boys have a permit for this rig?"

"Um, no," we'd usually reply.

"Well, you need a permit to use amplification."

"Where do we pick one of those up?"

"How'm I supposed to know?"

After a few more fines we had a stroke of luck when the boys from Agua Clara generously turned us on to quality intel on the matter.

"Bros, you go down to Midtown North and ask for Detective Cuomo in Community Affairs. He'll hook you up."

Turned out the permit was good for a five-day stretch between the hours of 10 AM and 10 PM but would also set us back $65 ($45 for the first day and $5 for each additional day). It appeared the right to amplified free speech was alive and well in the USA, as long as our wallets were deep enough. But we conjectured that with a little luck, we'd cover that nut on day one and use the rest of the week to turn a profit. Relieved to have finally unraveled the mystery, I double-timed it down to the precinct to score the elusive prize.

As I waited in the dilapidated, brick-walled lobby, a group of eight unlucky gentlemen daisy-chained together with communal hand-cuffs were led single file into the dismal holding tank at the back of the building. I found the humdrum, another-day-at-the-office demeanor of the cops overseeing the spectacle a little upsetting.

"*Weensteen?*" the desk sergeant called out, jolting me out of my anti-authority daydream. "Community Affairs will see you now."

After approaching the chin-level desk to obtain my building pass, I proceeded to the second floor, where Detective Cuomo interrogated me as I stood fidgeting in his dimly lit office.

"So, Mr. Weinstein, what exactly are we planning on doing out there?"

"Just singing and playing acoustic guitar, sir," I responded as unthreateningly as possible.

"And what type of music do you play?"

"Acoustic rock."

"You're not playing any heavy metal, right?"

"Yes. I mean, no. No, I don't play heavy metal," I verified, nervously pondering whether or not the genre had suddenly been outlawed.

"Okay, fill out this paperwork and display the permit when you are performing. Here's your receipt."

In parting he admonished, "And if you ever try to forge a permit, I will never grant you one again. Capiche?"

"Capiche," I replied and headed out the battered, grey, double metal doors, which banged and clanked behind me.

Standing outside the un-air-conditioned turn-of-the-century building, I excitedly examined my certificate:

This is a sound device permit to operate a loud speaker in connection with [Music Performer] Jed Weinstein at [Location] N/E/C – 58th Street & 5th Avenue. Not to exceed max volume of 85 db at ten feet. THIS PERMIT IS REVOCABLE AT ANY TIME.

We were learning how ultra-wary bureaucrats could be when it came to the power of the electrified soapbox—never mind that one of our founding fathers, Ben Franklin, viewed street performing as an effective tool for connecting with his neighbors and influencing popular opinion. He composed songs and poems and jammed in the town square. It is said that this experience was instrumental in forming his opinions regarding free speech.

Subsequently, whenever possible, we enjoyed shoving our hard-won slip of paper into cops' faces. Funnily, a lot of them had never actually seen one of these suckers before. They'd look at us inquisitively, as if it was something we'd cooked up in Photoshop.

Occasionally, the precinct even appointed us our very own cop to monitor the volume of our shows. He'd typically show up around noon, park his car directly behind us, and then, every twenty minutes or so, emerge to point his Breathalyzer-looking decibel reader directly at our amplifiers.

"Okay, take it down a notch."

Strum. Strum.

"How's that?" we'd ask.

"Play . . . Nope, no way, you guys need to lower down. I mean way down."

"Dude! The busses passing behind us are ten times louder than we could ever be." I'd heard classical musicians moan about a conductor riding them like a fascist dictator, but this was ridiculous.

Five months into a weekly groove that consisted of alternating between the pain-in-the-ass application process and rocking all-day shows, the city mysteriously began denying us access to performance spots. The permit had become an endangered species, and we couldn't figure out why. In addition, it was impossible to get Community Affairs on the phone to discuss the matter. About three weeks later, Detective Cuomo finally took one of my calls.

"Yes, hi. It's Jed Weinstein, how are you? I was just wondering if you could tell me which performance locations are currently available for musicians."

"How the hell should I know? I'm not a talent scout!" he barked.

"You know, Mr. Weinstein, this isn't friggin' *American Idol*."

"Whoa dude," I said. "Take a chill!"

We were never granted a permit again, though it wasn't for lack of trying. Somehow our applications (along with those of all the other street musicians) never made it to the top of the pile. Later on, we understood the full depth of the situation when Mayor Bloomberg sneakily implemented a campaign to privatize public spaces. He closed down the most traveled thoroughfares to car traffic and turned them into pedestrian malls. The city then rented out our former busking spaces for corporate events and weeklong promotions, charging megacorps upwards of $35,000 a day for the privilege. Why sell sound permits to broke-ass street artists for a paltry $65 when you could pull in crazy credit default swap-type Wall Street money for the same service?

At least we'd made an honest effort to go legit. Still, we had a ton of fight left in us and weren't about to let a development like this put an end to our blossoming music career. The show had to go on with or without—no, especially without—Big Brother's approval.

We likened busking to aural graffiti. It was our duty to scribble our sonic tag and spread outlawed musical seed wherever we could. Shit, if we had anything to say about it, the city streets would always be filled with jugglers, fortune-tellers, mimes, dancers, musicians, magicians, hula-hoopers, and clowns. With this in mind, we went back to feloniously blaring away on the avenues and back to getting ticketed. Only this time, we did what any good corporation does: wrote those pesky fines off as a business expense.

AS OUR CAMPAIGN continued, each plaza and walkway held out the promise of better cash flow and groovier acoustics, but with

9/11-derived security concerns as the excuse *du jour*, companies like Lehman Brothers and Reuters were fiercely protecting the perimeters of their buildings with concrete blockades the size of compact cars. Ultimately the city deemed this sort of thing illegal, but until then the behavior hindered many of our prospective money-making activities. On one occasion, I made the mistake of merely leaning against the Lehman Brothers building on Forty-ninth and Seventh Avenue and was summarily given the option either to leave the area or be arrested. Building security had seen my busking paraphernalia and was firing a warning shot. Being longtime skate rats, we were quite aware of these tactics, but being treated like terrorists was something we never did get used to. The harassment fueled our resentment, and we now relished utilizing the illegally privatized spaces for purposes never envisioned by their creators: smart-bombing their urban Frankensteins with our music.

WE WERE ALSO becoming familiar with the unwritten rules and customs governing the high level of commerce taking place on every street corner. Seemingly the entire populace was engaged in some kind of transaction, with people purchasing everything from fedoras, sunglasses, and I ♥ NY t-shirts (three for ten dollars) to cell phones and wallets. There were hot dog stands, Mister Softee ice cream trucks, and crêpemobiles. There were bagel and fruit carts, book peddlers, and merchants selling framed pictures of pop icons like Eminem and Kurt Cobain, and that classic shot of John Lennon flashing the two-finger peace sign in front of the Statue of Liberty.

"Where's the show today, rock stars?" William, a totally chill pashmina salesman, would ask as we passed on our daily spot-hunting ritual.

"Not sure yet," I replied. "Thinking we might hit Seventh Ave and Forty-ninth."

"Haven't seen you guys for a few days, thought you might have retired."

Now laughing: "Yeah man, I just won the lottery! Didn't I tell you?"

William gave us the lowdown on vending, explaining that most salesmen were Vietnam vets like he was—the only ones sanctioned by the city to vend on the avenues. They often sublet their permits in the same way a taxi medallion is shared among many drivers, building small dynasties in the process. It was a decent perk for having served your country.

In contrast, the Senegalese, who dressed in bright African caftans, dominated the city's black market. They were easy to spot from a distance; you just had to look for a horde of crazed tourists clawing over each other like a pack of rabid animals. They displayed illegal knockoffs of TAG Heuer, Movado, and Rolex watches from patent leather briefcases. This made for an easy getaway in the event of an occasional police sweep. To the chagrin of customers, sometimes in mid-purchase the case would be unceremoniously slammed shut, Bob and Edna from bumfuck left standing on the corner slack-jawed, while their sales associate sprinted down the street with their money still in his hand.

WITH ITS CLOSE proximity to Heth's apartment, Fifty-eighth Street and Fifth Avenue became one of our regular busking venues. More and more, workers from the surrounding buildings began spending their lunch breaks with us, accompanied by newly converted colleagues. When someone asked if we had any music to sell, Heth ran back to his apartment and grabbed a few boxes of the CDs we thought would never see the light of day, the same boxes that until then were being utilized as handy coffee tables and footstools. By the end of that shift we'd sold ten copies, substantially increasing the day's take. Later that evening I put my graphic skills to use, making a proper FOR SALE sign with a picture of the CD cover. With some fine-tuning of image placement, design, and price point, we began blowing through entire boxes and were eventually ready to do something we never thought possible: order more CDs!

Soon after our first CD sales, Paul, a six-foot-seven free speech activist and entrepreneur who could usually be found on the corner of Forty-fifth and Broadway selling LICK BUSH IN 04 bumper stickers, had a word with us. Turned out he was just itching to give us a copy of a letter from the Department of Consumer Affairs outlining exactly which items required a general vendors license.

"Yo guys, if the cops ever try to shut you down for vending CDs without a license, show them this. Fight the power!"

Thus, we learned that while a general vendors license (which, as Will had told us, was available only to honorably discharged veterans) is required for the sale of crafts and other merchandise such as figurines, incense, jewelry, clothing, and so forth, the sale of written matter, visual art, music, movies, items bearing political messages, and other First Amendment items, is exempt from this requirement.

Selling our discs united gobs of fans who could now readily share our music with their friends. And not only had we joined the throngs of merchants hawking their wares on the dirty boulevard, but we'd finally become bona fide professional musicians in the process. The results were swift, culminating in an entire lunchtime office crowd singing our song "My Headphones" back to us, word for word. We tried to act cool, like it was no biggie, but we were totally blown away.

My headphones still smell like your Chanel perfume and
You left your Springsteen CD in my room and
I miss your charges on my credit card 'cause
Living without you is just too damn hard

Then, one warm autumn evening, as the Broadway shows were letting out, dumping throngs of people onto the Times Square promenade, an enthusiastic bunch of Swedish kids plopped down on the skanky sidewalk to chill for our show. Soon everyone was doing it, until finally a crowd of hundreds was squatting in front of us. We'd somehow turned a quadrant of one of the most manic places on earth into an intimate living room complete with strangers clapping and grooving along like one big happy family. No small feat. After a few songs, people started lining up to buy our CDs, and within fifteen minutes we'd sold out. It felt great knowing the month's bills were paid, but even cooler, we'd banked a few places to crash if we ever made it to Sweden.

We seemed to be on a roll. At a show later in the week, our crowd grew beyond anything we'd ever seen before. With each extended guitar solo it tripled in size. Even the traffic on the avenue slowed down to watch us kick ass. People were shouting and hooting, some rode on the tops of vehicles like it was a parade.

Someone yelled, "Hey, you guys have power!"

We smiled back, with a nod. Then some crazy-eyed bald guy with a Marine buzz-cut descended on us.

"You two idiots are causing total chaos. Stop playing right now."

"Fuck you, man!" we retaliated. "This is a little something called rock'n'roll! Get used to it."

"Don't you know there's a fucking blackout? Get used to *that!*"

Thanks to our battery-powered show on wheels, we'd unknowingly become the house band for the Blackout of 2003.

OVER TIME, WE built up to playing six to eight hours daily, becoming privy to the city's changing moods. We carried on an affair of sorts, strumming for her as she awoke, yawning and stretching into a new day, then rocking harder in the afternoon, until we slid into bed with our mistress in the relative twilight.

We jammed through all kinds of shifts—swing, night, graveyard, and seismic. Afternoons contained the most insanity, jam-packed with stressed out, red tape–choked bureaucrats mostly rushing past without stopping. After a biblical exodus of office drones on their way back to the outlying bedroom communities, the mania dissipated all at once. Then, the Middle Eastern halal carts emerged, selling meats over spicy curried rice, filling the void of reasonably priced meals in midtown during evening hours. The later it got, the longer the lines grew, sometimes stretching down the block. This left us jamming amidst the lingering evening smog for tourists, pedicab drivers, cabbies, and wasted late night partiers.

Busking bonded us with the community in ways we never expected. "Heth-and-Jederz" hired us to play private shindigs, everything from baby showers and birthdays to Mother's Day barbeques. One guy even paid us a thousand bucks to set up in the wine cellar of a SoHo restaurant so we could ambush his girlfriend with their favorite song. As we played "Desert Sun," he got down on one knee and proposed. We were honored to be a part of that memorable occasion; luckily she said yes.

And what do I see? Looking through
You lift me up when the day is done
And what do I see? You know it's you
You warm me up like the desert sun

These days we walked the streets with our heads held much higher, finally contributing something to the world. No longer did we feel like orphans aimlessly adrift in Manhattan. We were becoming part of the cityscape and somewhat locally famous to boot.

"I love you guys," the bodega clerk said as I grabbed my morning café con leche. "My old lady and I are both big fans!"

"Thanks man, what's your name?"

"Carlos."

"I'm Jed."

"Yeah, I know," he said, smiling.

"So what's the damage, Carlos?"

"Nada man! Say hi to Heth for me."

Finally, with three hundred and fifty shows under our belt, we'd become the tight live band we'd always hoped to be. We matriculated through the University of the Streets, offering ourselves up as a sacrifice to the purifying fire of judgmental glare. The scrutiny forced us to evolve more quickly than if we'd been touring for a guaranteed paycheck, because if we missed too many notes in a row, the audience would grow impatient and bail on us.

Around this time, with meditation still a steadying force in our lives, Dan began teaching us Reiki, a Japanese energy-balancing method like Shiatsu. Without much forethought, we applied the ancient technique to performance, transmitting the energy of our music into the unsuspecting meridians and chakras of the public. We also took a cue from New Age heroes like Deuter, who composes top-notch healing meditation music, and from buskers like the Andean groups who douse their pan flutes in shitloads of atmospheric digital delay. By combining acoustic, electronic, and spiritual elements, we bathed our listeners in an uplifting wave of energy that, on a good day, could overpower the crush of midtown chaos.

With a couple of extra bucks in our pockets, we could now also afford to invest in the most up-to-date technology, and frequently stopped off at Manny's Music on Forty-eighth Street to check out the latest in guitar pedals. We picked up anything that looked promising, anything that could help us move our sound that much more toward the modern, dreamy, and interstellar.

We hit our stride after Heth bought a foot-controlled sampler called a Boss Loop Station off of Craigslist. The device allowed him to loop guitar and vocal parts as well as rhythm motifs on the fly, and in so doing, jam over the newly formed grooves. Though it took him awhile to tame that beast, it eventually doubled our audience size (and our salaries) and had the added benefit of helping our tiny duo sound more like a powerful four-piece band.

Looping became one of the hooks that enabled us to grow a fan base while playing only original music. By making fresh loops for each song, we were able to give the full experience of our recorded songs without a pre-recorded karaoke-backing track. After all this time, we'd finally connected the musical dots, creating a live show based on the Grateful Dead method of improvisation: state a theme and take it for a ride through the woods, using the technique we'd been hipped to all those years ago at the Kaiser Convention Center.

Our email list grew with each street show, but it was still mostly filled with out-of-towners. We'd proven our music had global appeal, but in order to accomplish our next goal of packing nightclubs, we needed to rally the locals, which meant relocating our roving rock concert underground.

ABOVE: First jam session in our new New York City apartment

LEFT: Hope and Heth around the time they first met

RIGHT: The tension is palpable right before the Airport Hug break-up

Mike Lonoff

ABOVE: Backstage at CBGB
BELOW: Playing CBGB, Heth on drums, Jed on bass/vocals

Mike Lonoff

5 October 1994

heth and jed Weinstein
New York, NY 10022

Re: Your demo

Dear heth and jed,

Well, here I am again writing you a letter. You said that you wanted some feedback so here are my thoughts. First of all I think the songs are very middle of the road. They are not strong enough to grab my attention and really hold it in the sense of production or lyrics. I don't feel anything fresh or new in them and you sound like you're just going through the motions.

I'm sorry, this is all probably not the type of feedback you wanted to hear but it's what I feel. The one positive thing I do have to add is that I like the sound of the singer..very distinctive and at times sincere. I don't know if you are the singer because it never indicates who does what on your tapes.

Thank you for this millionth opportunity to listen in on your lives. Please take my thoughts and make of them what you will and not as written law. I think you all have talent and just need to keep developing it.

Kind regards,

joe unger
Mercury Records, A&R

Mercury Records
Worldwide Plaza
825 Eighth Avenue
New York, NY 10019

a PolyGram company

Telephone: (212) 333-8000

Rejection makes you stronger

ABOVE: One of our first busking gigs on Fifth Avenue and Fifty-ninth Street

LEFT: Summer show in Times Square

ABOVE: 10 PM in Times Square is just as bright as 10 AM

OPPOSITE TOP: Jed keeping warm

OPPOSITE BOTTOM: New York City sound permit

THIS PERMIT SHALL BE CONSPICUOUSLY DISPLAYED DURING THE PERIOD OF OPERATING SOUND DEVICE

☑ FEE $ 65.00
☐ NO FEE

THE CITY OF NEW YORK

SOUND DEVICE PERMIT

133530

Note: Not to exceed maxium volume of 85db(A) at ten ft. 15min. prior to the start of the performance until the completetion, the decibel limit will be reduced to 75db at ten ft...

PRECINCT MTN

DATE OF ISSUANCE

New York 7/22 20 05

TO WHOM IT MAY CONCERN: This is a sound device permit to operate a loud speaker in connection with

Music Performer

at (location) N/W/C - 45th St. & Broadway on 7/24-28 20 05 from 10am M., to 10pm M.

at (location) ***************** on **** 20 ** from *** M., to *** M.

This permit is issued for the operation of the sound device above described, in connection with the event specifically mentioned herein. THIS PERMIT AUTOMATICALLY EXPIRES UPON TERMINATION OF THE TIME PERIOD STATED.

THIS PERMIT IS REVOCABLE AT ANY TIME.

Commanding Officer (Signature)

TOP: Heading to a Grand Central Station show; BOTTOM: Big crowd at the Staten Island Ferry Terminal

OPPOSITE TOP: In a Union Square groove;

OPPOSITE BOTTOM: Backstage shot at Eighth Avenue and Forty-second Street

ABOVE: Heth at Trout Studios, recording tracks for our album *Between the In and the Out*

LEFT: Overdubbing in Jed's apartment

OPPOSITE TOP: Cover of *Between the In and the Out*

OPPOSITE BOTTOM: Sound check at the Living Room

Between the In and the Out

High Tea at the Carlyle hotel, photo shoot for *Idress* magazine

Janice Muscio

9

Subway Series

[HETH]

Before our arrival in the subway system, the underworld was populated by tenderhearted folkies and sober classical guitarists. The sleepy sound of Peruvian pan flutes wafted on subterranean breezes. You never heard any screaming, in-your-face, Jimi Hendrix–style feedback. We'd entered some kind of rock'n'roll desert, a void in desperate need of a crunchy guitar riff.

Playing at the Union Square station was quite different from playing the concrete canyons of midtown, and each new station presented a unique set of acoustics to negotiate. While the mezzanines were like small stadiums, sound reverberating off tiled walls and metal support tresses, the smaller stations were akin to intimate clubs. And playing too aggressively anywhere created a jumbled, muddy mess that kept a prospective audience at bay.

Until then, we'd found it much easier to persuade a ticket-buying public to show up at a club than to pull a crowd from the ether. We quickly learned that to conjure a crowd, we had to become part showman and part shaman, striking classic rock'n'roll poses and then jumping around as though we were doing a rain dance.

With an eye toward longevity, we reorganized our set list.

Although it was financially beneficial to play the hits (any Bob Marley or top ten classic rock song would do), we decided to pass up guaranteed money, rededicating ourselves to performing our original material exclusively, hoping it would lead to a local grassroots fan base and packed shows at clubs. Occasionally though, we'd stave off tedium with our own twisted version of "Stump the Band," taking turns quoting lyrics from obscure songs. Whoever couldn't string the lyrics together on the fly lost the round. It was a cool way to reference our heroes and draw people in without compromising our "no cover tunes" pact.

Funny thing is, whenever we gave an audience what we thought they wanted, they abandoned us. So we quickly learned that the best policy was to stick with the vibration of the day. When we made a mistake, we went with it, falling into a vast gravitational pull, riffing on the discord until it spat us out the other end. When it felt right to jam on the same groove for fifteen minutes, we honored the impulse. Sometimes, after a fit of exploration, we'd call it all off mid-song, shards of sound exploding into dissonant gobbledygook, leaving our audience and ourselves befuddled. Other times, we pulled that spooky brother stuff, inadvertently ending songs together or playing unrehearsed, improvised lines in unison.

"Your voices really complement each other," listeners remarked, some not knowing we were related. We fantasized that maybe, in some small way, we'd joined the ranks of sibling groups who'd come before us: the Everlys, the Louvins, the Carpenters, the Beach Boys, the Gallaghers, all known for their unmistakable familial harmonies.

Our sound was evolving. People tagged us as influenced by late-'60s and '70s art rock acts such as Pink Floyd, Bowie, and early Genesis, laced with a blast of New Age ambience. We proudly wore these influences on our sleeve in hopes of attracting a local Heth and Jed army. And indeed, we soon realized we weren't alone; it seemed subway audiences were just as fed up as we were with the glut of low-grade, crappy corporate rock perpetually shoved down our throats via radio, television, and movies. When we played Yes and Zeppelin-esque riffs, former rockers, now forced to hold 9-to-5 cubicle jobs to be able to support their families, thanked us for "just being out here."

"Man, I haven't heard shit like this since I was in high school!" a fortyish guy in a suit and tie said while excitedly buying a disc. "Music is so horrible these days, I only stick with the classics."

"And us!" I added.

"Yeah, and you guys!" he laughed.

Encouraged by the public's response, we tapped into newly discovered reservoirs of stamina, often performing as many as ten shows in ten days. To pull off that final show we'd sometimes have to make a call to Dr. Feelgood, scoring gallons of coffee, multiple cans of Mountain Dew Code Red, and a shot or two of Jameson to smooth it all out. Because of our psychedelic sound, locals routinely dropped goodies in our case, especially when we played down at Fourteenth Street where the NYU kids hung out. Vicodin, Xanax, and joints aplenty ended up in our happy guitar case. One time, a guy we'd nicknamed Mushroom (he grew pounds of psilocybin in hundred-gallon fish tanks) came by to see if we needed any works. He said he'd just gotten some great heroin and would be glad to throw in some clean syringes gratis.

One of the coolest things we discovered was that we were often the first live musicians some people had ever heard. Young moms armed with designer strollers inched squirming babies toward us. Junior would hold a dollar bill while Mommy instructed, "Drop it in the case, honey." Out of respect for their virgin baby ears, we played ever quieter as they approached.

Another thing we had to get used to was how close everyone stood compared to when we'd played on the streets, often right up in our grills, audibly dissecting our performances. I found it unnerving, but I coped by telling myself they didn't know the real me. When that didn't work, I hid behind my bangs. One time, a woman watched for two hours straight—a long time, given that an audience typically turned over every few songs. Eventually, she trotted up with a big smile and tucked a buck in our case.

"You guys sound amazing," she said. "I know it's hard to be out here, but you gotta put more energy into your stage presence. Also, if you add more feeling to the vocals, it could mean the difference between playing at Penn Station and Madison Square Garden."

Normally, this kind of unsolicited advice didn't bother me, but being that we were into our fifth hour of playing and I was hallucinating, I had to call on all my years of meditation training to keep from kicking her in the neck. Instead, I mustered up a raspy, barely audible, "Okay man, thanks." Later that night, after dragging my tired ass home, I received an email from this Simon Cowell, Jr., further expounding on her earlier critique: "You should take acting lessons so that you can learn how to bring emotion into your singing and also consider getting a drummer." This is one of the hazards of being out there in public.

During those rough patches when it seemed like everybody and their mother was telling us we sucked, we employed a couple of patented responses, such as: "So does your mom!" And: "We'll be happy to refund your ticket, sir." Invariably, the former led to altercations involving our guitars and hecklers' heads. All that pent up rage from days of abuse would come pouring out and, wouldn't you know it, we'd find ourselves smack dab in the middle of one of the largest audiences we'd ever had. Only it wasn't the music-loving kind, more like the type that thirsted for blood. Consequently, we came to view the role of the busker as a reflecting pool of the human spirit. We were society's sewer and steam valve, punching bag and friend in a time of need, even its therapist.

One night, a thirty-something woman with short brown hair and gaunt features sat watching us from the wooden benches at Union Square. She seemed heavily burdened, so we waved her over. She approached with tears in her eyes, confiding that she'd just lost her father.

"Oh man, sorry to hear that," I said.

"I'm so happy to hear your beautiful music," she whispered. "I really needed this today."

But despite those wondrous moments, we still had dues to pay. A couple months later over at Grand Central, a flood of humanity was sweeping past when a tall, tweaked-out dude sauntered up to dance. We didn't think anything of it until he threw his hat down in front of our guitar case to catch our tips. We take that kind of shit very seriously, not keen on becoming anyone's backup band. If you ask, though, we'll give you some money.

To rectify the problem, Jed trotted up to the guy like a bass-playing Beckham and without missing a note, punted the tweaker's tip jar across the station. The dude went nuts, spastically waving his arms, and socked Jed in the throat. Not to be outdone, Jed plunged his bass into the guy's gut so hard it knocked him flat on his ass. (In a pinch, a bass makes a great weapon, thirty pounds of pissed-off rock'n'roll wood and steel.) Naturally, the audience was transfixed by the scuffle.

"He wasn't doing anything, man!" a kid in the crowd protested. "He wasn't bothering anybody!"

"Oh really?" I wondered into the microphone. "Well he was bothering me, motherfucker!"

Without roadies or security, we were forced to become our own bouncers. In time, we came up with a couple of proven ways to transform or disperse a tainted audience. Either we'd announce we were done for the day and feign tearing down, or we'd do a chakra sounding, the way we'd learned from our meditation teacher Dan, pumping waves of purifying *ohmmms* into the atmosphere.

Sometimes it wasn't the audience that was the buzz kill, but the cops. One Friday afternoon at Union Square, we had a huge crowd assembled, buying CDs, dancing, and cheering us on, when the boys in blue showed up. After surrounding us, they popped us for disorderly conduct and selling CDs. We protested, explaining that we were covered under the First Amendment (all the songs on the CDs were written by us), and besides, wasn't amplification legal here on the mezzanines? They were so accustomed to busting the CD and DVD bootleggers lining subway stations and street corners that they couldn't comprehend anyone actually selling their own copyrighted material.

"To start off," one of the cops said, "I'm gonna write you a ticket for violating decibel levels. I can't even hear my friggin' radio."

Our audience leapt to our defense. "Shame on you! Shame on you!" yelled one old guy. "Why don't you fuck with the rich people?"

In hopes of eliminating their subjective perception of our volume, I flipped it on them, demanding they read our decibel level. But my request only made things worse.

"If you have a problem, you can speak with my lieutenant!" the cop said, pointing to the door of the underground precinct, conveniently located a couple hundred feet away. I started to head over, but three steps into my journey, I was thrown face-up against the wall, my arm twisted into a pretzel.

"But I thought you said I could . . ."

"You got a big mouth!" the cop said, cuffing me with those thin plastic riot cuffs that grind into your wrists like razors. Tied up for what felt like an eternity, my fingers went numb. Satisfied he'd proven who was boss, he relented and let me go with fifty dollars in fines.

Things kept on like this for a while. Whenever we performed in a new location, we braced ourselves for the usual police hazing. But over time, as they became accustomed to our presence, we actually developed a pretty strong following among the NYPD. One of our biggest supporters was Donnie, a six-foot-three, three-hundred-pound police lieutenant who went so far as to stand outside our club shows with handmade artwork that read "Heth and Jed Rock!" in blue and red marker.

"Get in here! You guys gotta see this band!" he'd scream at passersby.

During concerts he double-fisted Budweisers, then, between songs, rallied our troops, getting entire audiences to chant "Heth and Jed! Heth and Jed!" Nervous bouncers were unsure how to handle our very large, boisterous, self-appointed number-one fan, and we were often called upon to console upset Heth-and-Jederz. "I love you guys, but that huge skinhead just tried to beat up my friend!"

The next day, he'd email us, *Guys I'm really sorry about last night. I'll try to behave next time.*

No way! Go as mental as you want, we always replied, ever the firm believers in partying until thrown the fuck out of any fine rock'n'roll establishment.

10

Breakin' 2: Electric Boogaloo

[HETH]

laying the subways was a revelation, a generally receptive environment in which to ply our trade . . . with one exception: We'd unwittingly been sucked into a turf war with several break dance groups. At first it seemed like a high price to pay for simply trying to get our music to the public, but we wanted in and weren't taking no for an answer. Until that point, the break-dancers had governed the most profitable, high-profile performance spots in the subway system, including Times Square and Thirty-fourth Street–Herald Square. They ruled these well-traveled, lucrative locales with such violence and intimidation that it rendered the areas completely off limits to outside performers.

We had initially approached these guys in a neighborly way, but quickly learned they weren't into negotiation, sharing, or collaboration for that matter. We had hoped to become friends with them, or at least forge a relationship based on mutual respect—something we currently shared with every other busker. After all, weren't we all brothers and sisters in busking? Unfortunately, they took our respectful overture as a sign of weakness, informing us that as "new jacks," we weren't allowed to play in their stations.

In busking etiquette, an empty spot indicates availability—first come, first served. But not in the breakers' book. It wasn't uncommon for us to stumble upon an open area and start up a show, only to have them pull in, outnumbering us four to one, and muscle us out. They'd customarily slide their tip bucket in front of our makeshift stage and move in to steal our audience. We would defiantly stand our ground, turn up our amps, and strum as loud as we could over the deafening strains of Michael Jackson's "Beat It" booming from their colossal PA system. Alas, we could never compete with their volume. A half hour into our volume war, the cops usually arrived and kicked every last one of us out.

Things worsened as the breakers continued their daily blitz, systematically banishing the competition to the lower-paying spots until we were the only ones left willing to take them on. A fellow busker who sings traditional Haitian-flavored songs said they had tossed her amplifier clear across the station during her last Thirty-fourth Street show.

After holding our own against the breakers for five tense weeks, we had one of our most violent encounters. We were serenading a crowd of about seventy-five people with our song "Walking Away from Heaven" when several guys in bright red hoodies, whom we quickly recognized as our nemeses in disguise, infiltrated the audience, lifting their shirts to expose the shiny metal of pistols protruding from their waistbands.

> *Then you see me*
> *But you can't be with me*
> *And then you tell me*
> *I'm walking away from heaven*

"Shit! *Gun!*" we yelled into our mics. We kept yelling it until the breakers scattered in five different directions. Once we calmed down and stopped shaking, we went back to work, making some good tips, selling more CDs than usual, but peering over our shoulders quite a bit.

These same idiots jumped Jed a week later over by Penn Station as he made his way back from visiting Mom in Jersey. They roughed him up and dumped a Big Gulp on his head. He was lucky to get away with only a few bruises and a fat lip. From then on, we watched our backs when walking in the train stations. Even on our days off we tread carefully now, with a heightened awareness of our surroundings.

We started bringing a camera to our gigs, too, which proved handy for documenting our adversaries' actions.

"I didn't say you could take my picture, motherfucker!" a wild-eyed breaker screamed during one of our next gigs, lunging at Jed, trying to pound his face in.

"Dude, we're not taking your picture," Jed said, dodging the guy's fists. "Welcome to YouTube, dickwad!"

Things spiraled further out of control when all the red hoodies joined in the fun, throwing Snapple bottles at our heads. The explosions of glass convinced normally passive bystanders to step in and call the police. When the cops came, they seemed freaked out.

"Are you guys serious?" they asked. "Do you really expect to take on all these guys?"

We could never figure out why the cops gave the break-dancers the run of the stations, until an undercover named Joe, who looked like a younger Sipowicz from *NYPD Blue*, complete with greased-back hair, mustache, and wife beater, spelled it out.

"Herald Square is gang territory," he said, his badge dangling from his neck.

"What do you mean?" I asked, as he nonchalantly picked up a switchblade left behind during the latest altercation.

"The break-dancers are in the Bloods, man. Nobody wants to deal with them, especially rookies. These guys are notorious for filing claims against us with the *Civilian Complaint Review Board*, and it stays on your record for good."

Everything started sloshing around in slow motion as I felt the weight of what we were up against. All I could think about was how Mom was going to kill me for getting Jed mixed up in all this. Until then, I'd merely seen our hoodied foes as competitive assholes bent on holding us back from a career in music. I guess that's what you get for growing up in the relatively placid Jersey suburbs.

Joe gave us his cell phone number, offering to be our "one call" if we ever got hauled in—a real live "Get Out of Jail Free" card.

"I love your sound, guys, been a big fan for a while. Keep it up!" he said as he bought one of our discs (employee discount, of course) before slipping back into the anonymity of the rush hour crowd. And we headed home, way too locally famous.

[JED]

I knew I'd been living in the city too long when I could tell the time of day using the skyscrapers as a Stonehengian sundial. I also knew that as soon as the towers prematurely blotted out the scarce Gotham sun rays, the break-dancers would migrate into the subway system from their usual outdoor summer spots at the Plaza Hotel and the New York Public Library at Forty-second Street to escape the winter freeze. Then the fight for high-end underground real estate would reignite.

While much of the summer of 2005 had been incident free, we weren't surprised when around twenty minutes into our first Herald Square set of November, a troop pulled alongside us, aimed their thousand-jigawatt sound system, and announced their presence by blasting us into oblivion. I have to hand it to them, they are a persistent bunch, and it was a pretty solid move. It left us with no illusions that their prime directive was anything other than *me first*.

Fed up with the constant harassment, Heth said, "You know what? Let's fuck with these assholes!"

"No, dude," I replied, trying to serve as the voice of reason. "Let's get the cops!"

"No fucking way. Remember last time, when the cops said they weren't our bodyguards? La, la, la, la . . . I can't hear you," Heth sang and stuck his fingers in his ears like a disobedient child as he skipped out into the middle of their dance party. I looked on helplessly. I knew from experience that his mess would soon be mine—the result of our sometimes inconvenient brotherly bond.

Audience members who'd witnessed the takeover stood up for us, yelling at the breakers, "Get the fuck outta here!" But a newly assembled group of hip hop devotees began booing and hissing big broski as he moved closer to the head break dancer, mimicking his every move. Like all good rockers, Heth was quite dance-challenged. Still, he did make a decent go of it, taking the opportunity to do his best Rockettes-inspired line dance with a dash of ska, mosh pit, and pogo thrown into the mix. Feeling left out, I joined in the fray. With our heavy combat boots, denim vests, long hair, and beards we stood out like two ex-con Busketeers.

At first, the breakers acted like they didn't care about the retaliation, ignoring us while yelling their customary call to arms: "Showtime! Showtime!"

We hollered, "No show! No show!" and made the guillotine gesture under our necks.

I admit our plan wasn't much of a plan at all, more like sketchy, improvised mayhem—but c'mon, we weren't going to just let them waltz in and take over, again. I was becoming more and more concerned about where this was heading, though, as all the commotion had attracted quite a sizeable crowd. Have you ever started down a path, and then couldn't activate the emergency brake or throw it into reverse even though you knew you should? Well, I figured, it was about time someone sorted this crap out once and for all, and it might as well be us. If we couldn't play here, we could at least make damn sure nobody else could, and, perhaps with the evil empire defeated, we would restore order to the busking universe.

But the dancers had a few more tricks up their sleeve. They announced to the predominantly black audience, "These guys are racists. They fucking hate black people!" We immediately felt the sharp glare of a hundred and fifty pairs of eyes bearing down on us as if we were wearing KKK hoods.

"We are not racists," we assured one and all. "We hate all assholes equally." Someone yelled, "Fuck you! You hillbilly motherfuckers ain't shit!" And just like that, it was on. A half-dozen spectators simultaneously lunged at us, scraping, gouging, and punching us until we were both pinned against a railing with nowhere to go but a thirty-foot plunge to the F-train platform below.

I could see the headlines: ANGRY MOB KILLS TWO STREET MUSI-CIANS AT HERALD SQUARE SUBWAY STATION. Yet somehow we were able to grab hold of our microphone stands and strike back, bursting into Zorro mode, yelling, "Back the fuck up!" With expert-ish swords-manship, we squirmed, slipped, and slid our way out from under the dog pile, then made straight for the station exit, regrettably with our bags already looted and our instruments stomped. Still not a friggin' cop in sight. *Where's the lieutenant when you need him?*

Despite a few scrapes and bruises, we were able to retreat unhin-dered, but not before the breakers got off a few parting gobs, their warm loogies adhering to our faces and hair like superglue. It wasn't until we safely hauled our mangled gear through the jail-cell styled entrance gate that we took a second to fully gross out. Several breakers followed close behind to convey a message: "Next time we see you bitches you're fucking dead. You hear me? Fucking dead!"

"This *is* next time, you assholes. Make your fucking move!" we replied while dousing our faces with Poland Spring. Hurling a stream of insults to make a sailor blush, they retreated, having won back "their" turf . . . for now.

IT WAS 3 AM when I speed-dialed Heth to see how he was doing. He answered, half asleep, "You okay?"

"Yeah man," I said. "I'm fine, but we gotta talk."

Deep sigh.

"I've been sitting here thinking about . . . you know, getting killed and stuff?" I said. "It's just that . . . well, I don't want there to be a hit out on me just because I want to play music."

"Yeah, dude. I totally agree. I've been thinking about it too, and I may have a solution to our problem."

The next day we stopped by the Bitter End in the West Village to have a beer and a word with a friend from the Planet Hollywood days. Mike was a four-hundred-pound, seven-foot-tall refrigerator of a guy who bounced for a few West Village clubs when he wasn't out protecting everybody from Puff Daddy to the Smashing Pumpkins. With a kid on the way, he'd given up touring in order to stick closer to home.

"Yo, Heth and Jed! My ol' pals!"

"Hey, Big Mike! How you been?" Big bear hug.

"Good man, real good. Did you see me in *The Sopranos*?"

"Yeah, man. Holy shit, congratulations! Hey, listen, do you think we can talk a little business?" He walked us into the bar. "Feel like making a few extra bucks next Wednesday afternoon . . . ?"

At our next gig, Heth and I brought along four hundred pounds of break-dancer repellent. Big Mike hung out on the side, standing with his arms crossed, while we rocked the house without incident. Several dance groups cased us but left after peeping our new sentry. Now everyone knew we had friends, too.

11

The Year of No Sleep

[JED]

eth called it his Year of No Sleep. The building next door to his apartment underwent a complete demolition that included jackhammering beginning every morning at 6 AM, which was when his bed began vibrating, and not in that hot and steamy, twenty-five-cents-for-five-minutes, hotel massage kind of way. Jarred awake, with nowhere else to go and feeling like a sleep-deprived Guantanamo prisoner, he grabbed his guitar and did the only thing he could.

Playing mornings was a whole different enchilada. Big bro had to shake the sleep from his eyes and learn how to complement the soft, dewy energy of a fresh new day, a universe away from the rock vibe we were cultivating as a duo. Noisier guitars had to be deferred until later in the afternoon; early morning subway audiences were comprised of exhausted commuters filing home after long night shifts and early risers groggily making their way to work, a Starbucks in one hand and the *Daily News* in the other. So, Heth concluded that to make it work, his sound couldn't be too jarring; it had to be more along the lines of what Bellevue probably piped into the mental ward to calm their guests.

Though Heth sported dark circles under his eyes, he was thankful the unyielding construction had at least been good for something. Besides forcing him to check out a new subway performance time zone, he'd made a few new friends, including Natalia Paruz the Saw Lady, a super-cool busker with long reddish hair and disarming smile who practices the lost folk tradition of making music with a carpenter's saw and violin bow.

Natalia and Heth often exchanged busking war stories. Once, she recounted how the police had issued her a ticket for possession of a deadly weapon, which forced her to have the saw's teeth filed off in order to continue playing in the subways. Fotunately, she said this hadn't affected the instrument's tone at all.

When performing, Natalia moves with a contagious joy, as if commanding a symphony. With each stroke of her bow and careful bend of the saw she extracts a melancholy sound, comparable to a bittersweet Billie Holiday vocal. Even though she has performed on prestigious stages such as Lincoln Center and alongside artists like John Hiatt and Zubin Mehta, Natalia is by far one of the most humble and hardcore buskers we've ever met.

We were also making friends with other subway musicians who, like us, persevered despite the logistical difficulties and hassles related to displaying one's talents in public. We first met Theo Eastwind when he was performing at the Sixty-eighth Street station as we waited for a downtown 6 train. A native of Austria, Theo moved to New York City in the mid '90s to run a Viennese bakery, but he fell into busking when the bakery lost its funding. New Yorkers' stomachs may have lost out on his sweet confections, but their ears gained an underground rock star. During his long decade of dedicated subway performance, Theo has encountered the usual difficulties arising from the lifestyle, including being arrested for selling his CDs. Following a degrading thirty hours spent in a jail cell, he hired an attorney and rallied against the city, standing up for his rights and winning a spot in every busker's heart.

Then there was Rashad. We could always count on Rashad to show up, grab a pile of our CDs, and begin hawking them to our Union Square crowd. He really helped our sales yet never accepted any commission for his big-hearted gesture. That's just how he rolled. Rashad was a fellow busker and a kindred spirit who had that Lenny Kravitz thing going on, having been born to an Italian father and black mother. He also sported long flowing dreads, and except for a deep scar on his left cheek, his face was sculpted like a Greek god's.

We usually saw him off in the distance, making the switch from the yellow to the green line, riding a perpetual loop from the Lexington and Fifty-ninth Street station down to Union Square and back again. He never played in the stations themselves, preferring instead to roam shirtless through the train cars, occasionally getting busted for illegally serenading riders with songs of love and unity, a tip cup dangling off the guitar neck to collect donations. I wholeheartedly believed the trains themselves needed a good energy balancing but didn't have the guts to play the subway cars. Heth tried a few times and said he felt like he was committing some kind of sacrilegious, intrusive act, as if contaminating the last remaining outpost of quietude in New York City. (Underground train cars are practically the only remaining spots in the city where cell phone reception is minimal and information overload gives way to old school, analog socialization).

Rashad insisted, "It's a hustle, man! That's what we're doing out here: We're hustlers!" When he spoke, he had this quirky way of cocking his head slightly to the right and peering at us from the corner of his eye. It made me wonder if he'd sustained some hearing loss from all the years of exposure to train noise, something we all had to look forward to, I supposed.

The one thing Rashad wanted most in life was a record deal. It was always, "when I get my deal" this, and "when I get my deal" that. By this time, Heth and I had cured ourselves of that affliction, or at least it wasn't our sole reason for rocking, yet we had no desire to dampen our comrade's enthusiasm.

"Just keep jamming, man," he always encouraged. "You never know who's out there listening . . . and no offense guys, but as soon as I get my deal, you ain't never gonna see my ass down here again."

It happens to buskers more often than you'd think. A big-time agent throws his card in your case or you get hired for a TV commercial, a bit part in a movie, or even chatted up by a strolling A&R man.

If you're out here long enough you end up declining plenty of offers too. We couldn't turn them down fast enough when Dunkin' Donuts approached us to participate in an ad campaign designed to promote their new 99¢ breakfast called "Breakfast NOT Brokefast." They offered us $20 an hour to not accept tips. Instead we were to display a sign in our guitar case that read, "Sure you want to throw that change in here?" We thought it was the height of disrespect.

We were offered another similarly disappointing opportunity when the rock band Oasis hopped the pond to promote their new album *Dig Out Your Soul*. Considering many buskers made Oasis songs staples in their repertoires, it was a no-brainer for their public relations firm to tap the street performer community. Many were willing to interpret the band's new songs in their own style and be filmed for the accompanying documentary, *Dig Out Your Soul in the Streets*, for the paltry sum of $100 each.

"Exsqueeze me?" we replied to the band's reps. "That's a lot of work. We can do it for $600."

"Are you crazy?" they laughed. "Everyone else is fine with the pay. You're passing up a massive opportunity here, plus you'll meet the band!"

It's not that we weren't big-time Oasis fans or that we didn't understand buskers were taking the gig as a *thank you* to Oasis for providing the material that helped them earn a living throughout the years. In fact we were front and center to see the band at the

Garden back in '94 at the height of the second British Invasion, but we couldn't rationalize being low-balled by a couple of rock stars who literally lived in castles.

Buskers are always on the cusp of dream fulfillment, inches away from breaking through to a higher level. Of course, I felt for Rashad; I understood his restlessness. I knew that subway performing could exact a heavy toll on your psyche. Early in our career, a veteran busker had ominously warned us that playing more than three days a week could damage us. Yet here we were, all of us playing daylong gigs as often as five days a week.

One day, Rashad dropped some heavy news on us. "Guys, I'm just not feelin' the love out here anymore. Performers ain't being appreciated the way they should be."

"Yeah, I hear you, man," we said.

"So, I've made up my mind . . . and I think I'm moving to Germany. Gonna be a black man in a white society for a while." As if to demonstrate his commitment, he pulled out his flight reservation. Rashad had fallen for a girl he'd met on MySpace and was moving into her Berlin flat at the end of the month. It happened just that fast.

We were more than sad to see him go. The three of us had forged a friendship under the severe conditions of public performance. Working the stations together had united us, allies in pursuit of free artistic expression. Yet, though we missed our older, more experienced brother, we were happy for him. His departure reminded me of what Dan had taught us many years earlier: that just staying in the game was half the battle.

Sometimes when I'm exhausted and strumming on autopilot, I see a faint hologram of our long lost brother strutting toward us, wearing his trademark ratty-ass guitar. We haven't seen Rashad in years and don't know if he ever received his record deal, but I do hope he knows how much his friendship meant to two fledgling dudes like us as we embarked on our first underground performances.

WE WERE BREAKING down our gear one day when we heard a familiar gravelly voice. Felipe, another fellow busker waiting for the spot, asked, "Guys, do me a favor? Don't pack up. My van just got broken into. Except for this one, every last one of my pan flutes was stolen."

"Wow, sorry to hear that, bro."

"Yeah and now my band just canceled on me. Any chance I could sit in with you guys?"

Eager to help out a fellow musician in distress, we said, "Sure, man. Jump in."

Felipe had a great tan and wore his hair in a couple of braids, one on each side of his head. "My girlfriend did them for me," he said. He'd crossed the country countless times playing a brand of Peruvian music that sounded like it had ricocheted off the highest peaks of the Andes about a thousand years ago, then bounced down to the present day. His standard garb was one of those ponchos like Clint Eastwood wore in *A Fistful of Dollars*. Every time I saw him, I thought, *Damn I've got to get me one of them things.* It's like when you attend a Renaissance Faire and find yourself with an inexplicable, impulsive need to own a cool wizard hat with trippy blue stars and bells. Then when you get home, you're like, "Fuck! I spent twenty-five bucks on this crazy shit?"

While jamming with Felipe, I noticed his fingers were adorned with thick silver and turquoise rings, and he was also sporting a large American Indian necklace that resembled the *Survivor* immunity idol.

"E minor, right?" he asked.

His trained ear quickly caught hold of the song's chord changes and he sailed effortlessly over our backup with a rocking flute solo. He kept us on our toes, bringing a whole new interpretation to our songs by playing some interesting passing tones we don't usually mess with. That's the beauty of music: It doesn't matter if you don't speak the same language or believe in the same invisible deity; art is the force that bridges all cultures and unites all people.

"You guys want?" Felipe offered, taking a swig from his vodka-filled Poland Spring bottle.

"Sure man." I took a drink and passed it.

"Yo, check it out, guys. This is a fifteen-thousand-dollar guitar that my boys in the Dave Matthews Band gave me when I worked on their last CD."

Felipe showed off that beaut like a proud papa. "Ever seen this kind of white pearl inlay in the shape of doves?"

After a few more sips he said, "Your music brings me such peace. It makes me want to close my eyes. I'm so tired fellas . . . so tired and I haven't slept in days. Keep on playing while I rest my eyes."

Felipe sat down on a milk carton in front of his trolley of belongings and drifted off to sleep while we continued the set. He slept for a long while, and when we tried to wake him, he couldn't be roused, so we tucked his cut of the take safely under his hat. We later heard he'd come out the other side of that weeklong binge only to discover that all his worldly possessions had been stolen yet again, including that sweet Dave Matthews guitar. About a month later, we noticed that Felipe had up and disappeared as well. At times, freedom can be an occupational hazard.

DURING HETH'S YEAR of No Sleep, Natalia the Saw Lady often played 9-to-12s at Union Square, arriving just as Heth was packing up, ready to retire upstairs to catch some Zs on a relatively quiet Union Square park bench before heading back to the construction zone that was his apartment.

"So are you and your brother auditioning for MUNY this year?" Nat asked him one day during the shift change.

"No, I don't think so," Heth replied. "We've already applied twice."

"Don't give up," she encouraged, a card-carrying member herself for many years.

MUNY (Music Under New York) got its start back in 1985 as a pilot program and after a great public reception it became official two years later. Sponsored by the Metropolitan Transit Authority, its goal was to beautify the subways and bring a measure of warmth and civility to the stations. MUNY also strived to reflect the diversity of the city's culture by organizing more than one hundred and fifty free shows weekly with a roster of over one hundred artists, everyone from Senegalese kora players to flamenco guitarists, as well as jazz ensembles and opera singers.

As far as we were concerned, MUNY was literally handing out record deals. If we passed the audition, we'd be one of the few hand-picked acts openly permitted to perform at more than a dozen monthly scheduled performances. Spots were located in the most highly visible and busiest locations in the subway system including Times Square, Union Square, and all the commuter railway lines (Long Island Rail Road, New Jersey Transit, and Metro North). Though we'd receive no salary or free entry into the stations, the main benefit would be a reduction in the number of amplifier-related police hassles and turf wars. But, best of all, we'd have a guaranteed spot waiting for us when we left our cozy apartments.

Prior to the 2006 round of auditions, rumor had it that MUNY was looking for musicians who were more soothing than rocking. In past years we'd unsuccessfully submitted videos of our duo jamming in Times Square, so we decided to rethink our tactics. This time we recorded a less bombastic video of Heth playing solo and demonstrating his freshly minted, smooth morning, subway platform yacht rock. Dressed in a black suede suit jacket, nicely shaved, and with his hair pulled back into a ponytail, he looped a flourish of guitar riffs and solos that were heavily drenched in his now signature spacey echo. Since we knew that selected musicians were sometimes allowed to perform with collaborators, we hoped Heth would gain access as a soloist and then, by default, hoist our duo into the fold.

Eureka! Third time was the charm. Heth received a letter of invitation to the auditions held annually at Grand Central Station. It read, "Please come audition on May 10, 2006, from 9:00 AM to 9:05 AM." He'd have five minutes to impress a discerning panel of judges composed of MTA station personnel, veteran MUNY buskers, and other professional musicians from the classical, jazz, and rock worlds, as well as a smattering of faculty and performers from local cultural institutions such as Juilliard.

Heth wanted to pass the audition so badly he could taste it, but he was up against some seriously stiff competition. Out of hundreds of applicants the field had only been narrowed down to about sixty prior to the auditions. We planned his strategy: He'd arrive at Grand Central mega early and set up his gear without rushing, making sure all his pedals, cables, and neurons were firing properly.

But before he knew it, he was being introduced: "Ladies and gentlemen, please welcome Heth Weinstein. It says here, he's a *one-man electric band.*"

[Applause.]

Awesome! A very friendly audience.

The warm reception melted Heth's nerves and he began layering down a tight rhythm track complete with funky bass line played on the low D string. He then pounded in a drumbeat using the palm of his hand on the outer shell of his guitar. The loop circulated throughout the hall's atrium, bouncing off the elaborately decorated ceiling, then back down to the finely buffed marble floors. After a few more guitar riffs he capped off that puppy using his Ebow. The Ebow, a brand name short for electric bow, is a hand-held, battery-powered device that vibrates the strings of a guitar via electromagnetic pulses, producing a sound reminiscent of a violin bow.

[Enthusiastic applause!]

Although he was unsure how well he had done at the audition, a month later the acceptance letter arrived. Natalia swore she had nothing to do with it; however, I believe she was his guardian angel. Heth and I threw a little shindig to commemorate the happy occasion. Surrounded by close friends, and with a few potent joints of Pineapple Kush making their way around the room, a rag–tag assembly of musician pals took turns belting out tunes in a scene reminiscent of our folks' Los Angeles dinner parties of yore.

Strangely, out of the twenty or so musicians accepted into the MUNY class of 2006, only a few rugged souls stuck with the program. It may seem counterintuitive, but prior to auditioning, many acts had never even attempted busking. They weren't aware of what one has to endure before playing even a single note: hassles like transporting massive amounts of equipment up and down a shitload of staircases and cramming into overcrowded trains brimming with severely pissed-off commuters. Then there's the difficulty of making a buck in freezing temps or stifling hundred-degree heat. On broiling summer days, there's no breeze and the air is so muggy that within minutes your clothes are completely soaked with perspiration. Couple this with bad money days and deafening train screeches, and you get a dropout rate of titanic proportions. On those bleak days, the key to long-term busking survival is heeding the sage advice of our comrade Theo Eastwind: You have to go out every day to catch the good ones.

12

Cosmic Intake Valve

[JED]

As official members of the Music Under New York program, we now had a partner in crime. All we needed was a great new product to sell. That's where our old bud Jamie Candiloro came back into the picture. Since we'd last worked together he'd been drafted into the majors to record with such killer artists as R.E.M. and Ryan Adams. But he hadn't forgotten about his pals, the subway rats.

Jamie said, "Whenever you guys are ready to make the next record, I'm totally there for you." Heth and I took him up on his offer, and together we began preproduction. At one of our first meetings, JC turned us on to a book called *TuneSmith: Inside the Art of Songwriting* by Jimmy Webb, the guy who wrote classic songs like "Up, Up and Away" and "MacArthur Park." It completely rocked our world and helped us gain a new understanding of arrangement, melody, and lyrics and set the bar much higher for our next batch of tunes.

But before we could begin recording, Jamie also suggested we road test prospective songs, which meant taking full advantage of the, ahem, honesty of New York audiences. After about six months, we narrowed the field down to the top nine of the twenty or so new songs that consistently attracted the most listeners, tips, and hugs. Finally, a track listing for the CD was born.

We consider recordings to be markers in time with each song, an aural snapshot of a band's headspace on a given day. So we were anxious to finally record the new sound we'd been developing, particularly the ambient/psychedelic vibe that surfaced most prevalently in songs like "Up at the Farm" and the title track, "Between the In and the Out." But due to excessive volume and my apartment's thin sheetrock walls, recording drum tracks at home was out of the question. So on a crisp October morning in 2005, we packed all our gear onto the F train and headed over to Park Slope's Trout Studios to lay down the basic rhythm tracks (bass and drums). Heth was slightly concerned about his rusty timekeeping abilities. He hadn't picked up a pair of drumsticks in nearly two years and feared the day might turn into an expensive disaster. However, under Jamie's killer guidance he was able to relax and ultimately conquer the basic tracks in a few hours. "Like riding a bike," he later bragged, forgetting about the prior two-week period spent at Ultra Sound Rehearsal Studios busting our asses to get back into the tight little Airport Hug rhythm section we once were.

One great irony of the modern musical age is how the same digital Pandora's box that recently devalued music and derailed the music business gravy train ended up becoming the salvation of countless independent musicians. Even though we wanted to stay connected to a world where music is real, not manufactured by the corporate machine, and where a music career is based on sweat and blisters, not instant fame and Photoshop, we took full advantage of every technological recording advancement we could. Once the drums were done, recent breakthroughs in home recording made it possible to get professional sounding results while tracking in a relaxed apartment setting.

Back in Los Angeles, Jamie edited our tracks, then uploaded them to an FTP site (a method of transferring files too big for email). With files in hand, or rather, loaded onto my gooseneck-screened iMac Cube (outfitted with a pirated version of Digital Performer) we spent the next seven months overdubbing guitars, synths, and vocals in my one-room shoebox on Clinton Street. Since we were self-financed, we couldn't miss a day of our regularly scheduled busking shows, which made for some delirious yet mighty warmed-up after-work vocal performances. Without any deadline pressure or recording label breathing down our necks to create easily digestible three-and-a-half-minute ditties, we took full advantage of our creative freedom and indulged our burgeoning fascination with songwriting and digital recording. I think Yahweh was looking down on us too, because we didn't collapse from exhaustion, and not one of my neighbors complained about all the late-night vocal takes.

There was admittedly one hiccup in the process when it came to packaging our new album. At one of our recent shows, we'd met a friendly photographer named Go.

"Hey, I'll photograph you guys for free," he offered, his mega-expensive, megapixel camera hanging from a string around his neck. "I'm looking to shoot some bands for my portfolio."

"Good timing, man—we're actually looking for a photographer to shoot our new CD cover. But please, do not pass Go, and do not collect two hundred dollars," I joked. Go was a recent Vietnam émigré, so when he didn't laugh at my lame attempt at humor, I flattered myself by assuming it had to do with a possible language barrier between us. Nonetheless, he smiled respectfully.

On the day of the shoot, we met down at our agreed-upon spot in Chinatown, below East Broadway. I think we were on Henry Street when the hundred-year-old arched brick supports of the Manhattan Bridge caught Go's photographer's eye.

"Guys, why don't you hop that fence and we'll get some nice shots underneath the bridge?"

"You mean that fence over there with the sign that clearly reads NO TRESSPASSING?" I clarified.

"No, no, don't worry. I've been in there before," he assured us.

So over we went—Go with all his state-of-the-art cameras, and us with our instruments. We climbed onto a pile of twisted metal and threw our guitars on for effect.

Snap, snap, snap. "Smile!" *Snap, snap, snap.*

"Hold that thought," I said. "Gotta drain the lizard."

I was protected from view on all sides except—I noticed too late—for a slight gap opening out onto the street. When a taxi crept by and all three passengers glared at me, I shot them a knowing look. *Fucking perverts.*

They disembarked, hopped over the fence and made straight for us. Our hearts were pounding in our throats as we wondered who the hell they were, a possible Chinese triad? Had we stumbled onto one of their secret hideouts?

"What are you guys doing back here?" they asked.

"Taking band photos," we replied.

"You shouldn't be back here."

"No problem, we'll leave." We grabbed our stuff and headed for the gate but the trio pulled police badges from under their shirts.

"Hands behind your back."

"For what?"

"Public urination and trespassing."

The next time we met up with Go it was a month later at 7 AM in front of the courthouse. He was acting real peculiar, not at all his usual happy-Go-lucky self. Turned out he felt we had shamed him. By the time the judge was done with us, the free photo shoot had cost us around two hundred bucks each, plus court costs. On top of the fines, I was also kind of embarrassed, since the night before

I had googled "public urination" and found out it was considered a sex crime in several states.

NEVERTHELESS, WE NOW had a sweet, sweet set-up as we freely bounced between subway and street gigs, playing our allotted MUNY spots, then finishing up on the breezy avenues. We were enjoying the greatest creative autonomy of our lives, traversing Manhattan unreservedly, capitalizing on the venerable tradition of rocking out all day and night, logging invaluable performance time, selling mega numbers of our new disc, and meeting awesome people from every corner of the globe.

Once, we saw a woman, elegantly decked out in a bright shawl and carrying a bouquet of roses, being chauffeured down the wide Fifth Avenue sidewalk in a wheelchair. Before we knew who she was, we already felt we were in the presence of royalty. With a blanket over her legs, hands folded, eyes sparkling crystal blue, she sat regally motionless, listening to us play. At the end of our set, her assistant, the clean-cut guy in his mid-thirties who had been wheeling her along, came over grinning and whispered, "That woman right there is Fay Wray. She was the star of the original *King Kong* and she's mesmerized by your music."

"Like . . . wow! That is so frickin' awesome!" We looked over with a smile and bowed to her. I've never had the inclination to bow to anyone before or since, but when you meet the love of King Kong's life, the ninety-something-year-old Queen of Scream, you just do the bow, man. Before they left, she sent the assistant over to give us each a rose. We felt lucky to have played for her majesty mere weeks before her passing. When she died, they dimmed the lights on the Empire State Building for fifteen minutes. RIP, Fay.

We hobnobbed with a few other legends, too. It must have been at least a hundred degrees in the direct sunlight when rock legend

Patti Smith came strolling by while we jammed on the corner of Fifty-ninth. Heth was hitting some serious power chords when she gave us a wink. "Rock on, Patti!" we shouted. We later found out she had done some busking early in her career, along with sleeping on the park benches located only a block or two from where we were presently throwing down.

I think Heth must have a famous people radar detector built into his brain. It doesn't matter if we are jamming or being mugged, he can always spot a celebrity. Like the time Donald Sutherland was our guest at Forty-seventh Street and Broadway. Heth was so star struck he yelled into the microphone, like a total doofus, "Hey, Donald Sutherland in da house!" Donny boy smiled back, but made a hasty exit once he realized he'd been outed in front of a busload of salivating Midwestern tourists.

The time Mick Jones of Foreigner happened by (not to be confused with Mick Jones of the Clash, which would have been equally cool), Heth and I kept glancing at each other to confirm that what we were witnessing was actually real. Were we seriously playing for the God of Rock who'd written "Hot Blooded" and "I Want to Know What Love Is"? When we finished our song, he came up and tried to buy a CD. We said, "No way, man! This is for you, for all of your amazing music." Then he shook our hands and dropped a twenty in our case anyway.

Once, we were having a bad money day over on Seventh Avenue, mostly due to the cold weather (we'll generally pack up and go home at around thirty-seven degrees). Despite the fingerless gloves we had on, our hands were stiff. Our amps and guitars were brittle, making it all the more difficult to connect with an audience. Suddenly Heth's famous people detector went off again when all six-foot-five of Mick Fleetwood sauntered by in a pimped-out fur coat. I followed him across the street and tried telling him how much I loved his music, before forcing one of our CDs on him, but found myself tongue-tied in his presence. He was way gentlemanly about it, helping to decipher my disjointed grunts.

"So you want to give me your CD . . . right?" he asked.

"Y-y-yes, Mr. F-F-Fleetwood."

"Cool, man! I'll listen to it on the plane."

And then there was the time that Bob Dylan walked by as we played Eighth Avenue. I nearly fainted but Heth took off his guitar and went running down the street after him. For a second there it looked like he was going to make contact with Mr. Tambourine Man, but when he got too close, Bob's companions went all human-barricade on him.

Heth asked, "Can I at least give him our CD?"

"Nope! Now get outta here."

I'm sure everyone and their mother wanted a piece of Dylan but hey, it was worth a shot.

Oh! And there were famous people in the subways too, but it was a whole different vibe. On the streets, stars jumped in and out of limos shielded by their extensive entourages, but taking the trains was more of a solitary pursuit. Tobey Maguire once rolled up with his kid in a stroller and placed five bucks in our case, then took in the show. No hat, no sunglasses, and still nobody knew who the hell he was—sometimes the best disguise is no disguise at all. We also met one of Heth's all-time musical heroes, Rod Morgenstein, the drummer for the Dixie Dregs and illustrious Berklee College of Music professor. After he threw some cash in our case, Rod smiled, then bolted down the steps toward the arriving 6 train, but not before Heth could thank him for all the life-altering tunes. We met and became friends with bass goddess Greta Brinkman, a serious badass who's toured with such artists as Moby and Debbie Harry. And we can't forget meeting Max Weinberg, drummer for Bruce Springsteen and Conan O'Brien's *Tonight Show*. We were in the middle of a particularly rocking version of "Falling Together" (if we do say so ourselves) when we spied Max heading for the L train. Heth literally dropped his guitar mid song, ran over to his idol, and shoved a CD into his hands.

Are we falling together?

Are we stronger than ever?

Are we gonna make it through the night alright?

"Hey Max, you're the fucking man!" Heth gushed. "So do you guys ever give local bands a shot? You know, like us buskers? Maybe tell Conan to have us on the show some time." Heth might have been a little aggressive, but seriously, what the hell were we doing out here in the bowels of New York City if not pushing our music on everyone and anyone that could possibly help our cause? After the assault Max looked slightly miffed but shook Heth's hand nonetheless and said, "I'll see what I can do."

After meeting stars, I usually fantasized about what it would be like to perform all over the world, in venues other than windswept avenues and dank subway stations. To be transported into the lap of luxury, packed stadiums, guaranteed paychecks, and the world of swanky green room deli trays. I allowed myself that minute of fantasy before wisely shaking off the daydream and going back to working within our circumstances—something Dan had taught us how to do in spades. He instructed, "The best way out of a situation is into a situation." We applied his teaching as best we could, filtering it through the prism of street performance.

Maybe it was our latent messianic complex kicking in, but we came to view busking as a genuine act of shamanism, and ourselves as intermediaries bridging spiritual and physical planes. Show after show, a strange and powerful energy visited us, turning us into junkies for the addictive current of what felt like otherworldly support. We acted as a musical air purifier—a cosmic intake valve removing harmful psychic pollutants from the collective commuter psyche—and it hasn't left us since. So as not to piss off the gods of inspiration, and to keep the creative energy flowing, we made sure to keep careful records of any subconscious messages, song ideas, or guitar riffs that came to us under the influence of this energy.

THOUGH WE'D COME a long way, there were moments when I was forced to defend my lifestyle. I remember making out with a hot chica in the back of Motor City Bar on Ludlow Street; when the busking subject came up, she exclaimed, "Hey, I'm sorry but I could never be with someone who performs on the streets. What would I tell my friends?" Bam! She gulped the remainder of her appletini and bolted.

The first couple of times this happened I was blindsided, thinking it was an anomaly, but when it happened a third time, and then a fourth, I briefly entertained the notion that busking might be a shameful disorder. I wondered if my demonically possessed soul was in need of an exorcism. When I went out with new women, I wrestled with whether I had to divulge my dark secret right away, or if I could wait a few dates first.

I practiced my rap in the mirror. "Busking is not begging. Our hands are not simply outstretched. It's a trade, as in we trade our music for money . . ."

I eventually came to the conclusion that some folks didn't get it and probably never would. Unless we somehow became media darlings, we'd hover forever just below the threshold of general acceptability.

"Heth and Jed?" a co-worker from the Planet Hollywood days inquired, stumbling upon our rock'n'roll show. "What the hell are you two doing out here? You guys aren't homeless, are you?"

"Homeless?" we exclaimed. "Nah . . . just rockin' the fuck out, dude! Promoting the band."

Another time we tried to get the attention of one of Heth's high school exes as she fought her way through midday foot traffic. They were hot and heavy for a while back in eleventh grade. Even so, when their eyes met in recognition for the first time in years, she hastily cupped a hand around the side of her face and made the I-do-not-fucking-know-you gesture.

Except for these few glitches in the matrix, we were experiencing a surge of support like we had never felt before. The people of New York City had shown us so much love, and Music Under New York had finally welcomed us aboard. Family and friends were stoked for us, too (with the caveat that Mom and Hope were always warning us, "Stop playing at Herald Square, it's too dangerous!")

Run-ins with our nemeses the break-dancers aside, busking had become our all-around remedy for bad moods, since shows left us feeling more balanced—at times as if we'd received a four- or five-hour hug. Especially once we began the practice of posting our gigs on our website—after that, we routinely had crowds waiting for us when we arrived at our scheduled spots. Some days it was fans from Canada, or maybe a bunch of local Fashion Institute kids. Other times, folks beamed in via satellite hook-up, like the time our friend Amber stopped by and held her phone up for the entire set so her boyfriend, the self-proclaimed biggest Heth and Jed fan in all of Italy, could get his fix. "You guys know how addictive your sound is, right?" he told us.

Thanks to the diversity of New York City crowds, we had gone international. Apparently, we had no real need to tour, since the world routinely came to our doorstep. While most bands strained for international exposure, we were frequently written up in such faraway places as Brazil, India, and Israel, all by people who'd come across us during their travels. We often received emails from international fans well in advance of an impending visit: *Hey guys! We are huge fans visiting from France at the end of June. We'll be coming to all your shows. Can't wait to see you two!* We were honored by the repeat business of folks who made us a regular stop whenever they were in town; that's how we learned that busking was an international phenomenon and much more accepted overseas. In fact, we weren't even familiar with the term "busking" until one of our European audience members used it in conversation!

It's funny what sticks with you. I'll never forget the time we surveyed our audience and noticed a group of people listening attentively, all sitting on folding chairs. We later learned they had been moving around the tubes all afternoon, catching various street performers. As they say, "only in New York."

I knew we were really blowing up when I earned my very own stalker, in my very own apartment building. Eve would have been proud. I finally understood what the hell she'd been going through. Whenever I came home, my shirtless neighbor opened his door and stared me down like he wanted to rape or kill me, or perhaps both.

"Hey dude. I know who you are. You're in Heth and Jed," he said. "I like your band a lot. You're not as good as my band, but you guys are good."

"Really? What band are you in?"

"Well, I'm not really in any bands . . . anymore," he said, clearing his throat. "I mean I've grown up. I have an adult job now."

Another problem was he was always home, twenty-four-fucking-seven. It was difficult living in the adjoining apartment as he monitored my every move. When I arrived home exhausted after my shows, the shirtless wonder popped his door open and interrogated me.

"I heard you getting busy last night. Was she at least cute?"

I knew his entire routine too, including his familiar cough and how he liked to talk to himself, until, like clockwork, every night around 4 AM he'd blast Norwegian death metal while smashing the adjoining wall with a metal pan, screaming, "Jed, I'm gonna fucking kill you, bro. You're a fucking dead man!"

The next day he'd repent, leaving freshly baked chocolate chip cookies or a giant batch of brownies in front of my apartment door, accompanied by a note that usually read something like: *Hey man, here are some goodies to help you recharge those creative juices. Enjoy! P.S. I heard you working on that new song yesterday, really nice!* Of course I handled his "gifts" with a surgical mask, hazmat suit, and salad tongs.

My landlord and the cops were no help at all. The one time I went down to the local precinct to file a complaint, they made veiled homosexual jokes about me having a male stalker. Things really escalated when Heth came down to have a word with Creepy McGee (the nickname some other tenants in my building gave him). When he arrived, he was still pumped from an earlier busking show during which gang after gang tried to oust us from our lucrative Grand Central spot. We hadn't been able to get through a single song without defending our terrain, despite our MUNY permit. Too bad ol' Dale McStalkerson made the mistake of blocking the hallway as we loaded in.

Smashing his shoulder into Heth: "Watch where you're going, fucking asshole."

"What did you say?" Heth asked.

"I said, watch where you're going or I'll kick your faggot ass."

Before I could say anything, Heth pulled him down the staircase and pinned him against the wall, jabbing his trusty five-foot metal microphone stand under his neck. (I swear Heth is having a love affair with that thing; it really is his implement of choice when he needs to make a statement.)

"You got some kind of fucking problem with my brother?"

"No man," he gurgled. "No problem here."

"Well, from now on, if you got something to say, you say it to me. Got it? Don't even look at him or I will fucking end you!"

"Yeah, man. Okay, calm down."

"Now get the fuck back into your hovel!"

As I watched Dale limp upstairs and obediently close his apartment door behind him, I figured this must be why God had invented older brothers.

13

Fat of the Land

[HETH]

We were playing Times Square and kicking butt. Besides good tips and CD sales we also received a bunch of consumables. It all started when a guy in full Body Glove workout garb dropped five ZonePerfect nutrition bars into our guitar case. By the end of our song, he'd changed his mind and added another handful to the pile.

"You guys sound great. Eat 'em up!"

During our next tune, one of our regulars dropped a bag of Snapple iced tea into our case. Score! Before the show was over, someone else had chucked a few Hershey's bars on top of our growing cash pile. *Shwing!* It was a full-on diabetic smorgasbord.

"I don't have any food to give you guys," a girl with a hot Norwegian accent explained, "but I'd sure like to get one of your CDs."

"Step into our office," we replied, with a one-liner from our expanding arsenal that would have made Dad proud. (While we had barely made contact with him in years, thoughts of Dad surfaced all the time—whenever we heard the familiar sound of his belly laugh emanating from one of our own pie-holes, or in that occasional moment when we yearned for fatherly advice.) In any case, it was as if, through busking, the community had come to our aid, finishing our parenting and maybe even turning us into (God forbid) fine young men.

All the support that day was particularly gratifying since just a few days earlier we were taunted by dark energies as we tried out a new spot hundreds of feet beneath the crust of Times Square. To keep things fresh we try not to perform in any one location too frequently; otherwise we risk infecting the public with a severe case of Heth and Jed overload. We often let spots lie fallow while rotating newly discovered locations into the ol' performance roster. Years ago, a marketing study was conducted that revealed New Yorkers rarely stray off a set daily route, which probably explains why we see the same faces at the same spots again and again. (It also explains why a Starbucks can open up directly across the street from another Starbucks without impinging on the latter's business.)

We took the elevator and felt ourselves going down, down, triple down into the bowels of Hades. (Just make your first left at the bottomless pit, then turn right at the Lake of Fire.) Every spot we play has a unique personality, and when we arrived at the bottom of the Times Square pit, both of us had the sneaking suspicion that this one was going to suck. Having made the trek, we shook off the negative vibrations and gave the place a chance to prove us wrong, but it only took us fifteen minutes of playing before we had this puppy pegged: demonically possessed insane asylum.

Besides the garbage strewn all over the place, the station floors were covered in a slippery film of soot. A family of rats was scurrying along the walls, darting in and out of a drainage pipe from which an unidentifiable liquid had been dripping long enough to form stalactites. Without windows or any sense of direction, we couldn't help feeling somewhat claustrophobic, trapped in a confusing underground labyrinth. I pray it never occurs, but I'm positive the day will arrive when a terrorist attack hits the subways. I can only hope they take us out while we're cranking a kickass rock show so we can die with our boots on and not have to claw our way through mounds of apocalyptic debris.

Down in the hole, Jed and I refocused and got ready to rock, kicking out the first song of the afternoon, "Sunday Driver." We threw ourselves balls-deep into the jam, making our best effort to gather an audience here on the abyssal plain. All kinds of undiscovered species paddled by. We had visits from more common specimens as well, such as the ever-present scraggly drunk (*Drunkulus vulgaris*) in the front row who danced and shouted, "Work that shit! Work it!" All his yelps and whoops were helping build us a crowd so we let him carry on for a while, with the hopes he'd soon split town, until . . . *boom!* It all went haywire. The motherfucker whipped out his johnson and started jerking off to the groove of our jam. With his giant member dangling, he went for a trifecta and released his testes from their burrow, no doubt enjoying the full scrotal freedom.

Audience members had not yet discovered the complete range of wonders awaiting them until he began squirting urine. At first, everyone thought he was just spilling beer, but like a feral dog marking his territory in spurts, he shot a yellow stream a good eight feet (must have taken his vitamins). His warm droplets rained onto our jeans and amplifiers. A bunch of well-dressed business people and some emo kids ran for cover.

"You sick motherfucker!" we barked, trying to protect our equipment. "Now get the hell outta here!"

The bitter stench of the pisser's discharge filled our nostrils. With no sense that anything was amiss, he wallowed there for a while with his member still exposed, trying to chat us up. Turned out he was quite the music aficionado, too.

"C'mon boys! Play something good!" he demanded. Thank God he'd taken a special liking to Jed and not me. "Yo, you're the shit, Mr. Bass Man!"

Jed said, "Thank you, sir. But could you please put your dick back in your pants?"

Out of the corner of my eye I spied two cops approaching, each pulling on a pair of those there's-no-way-in-hell-I'm-touching-you tight leather gloves. Salvation at last, as our heroes scooped up the pisser and whisked him out of the station. "I don't care," he said, fading out of earshot. "Do whatever you want to me. I got AIDS. I'll be dead soon anyway!"

As if lining a puppy cage, Jed grabbed a few newspapers from the overflow of a nearby garbage bin and covered the steamy puddles the pisser had left behind. While slathering on gobs of the Purell we kept stashed for just such occasions, we tried cheering each other up, joking that a regular 9-to-5 was looking pretty sweet right about now. We eventually regrouped, playing a while longer, but our hearts weren't exactly in it, plus the area reeked to holy hell. Our busker's intuition had been one hundred percent accurate: This spot sucked.

IT WAS THIS kind of occurrence that reinforced our general belief that our band operated a world away from the more civilized club atmosphere where public urination is not a hazard of the job, and performers frequently demand silent, attentive crowds for their music. Once, after a long, hard day of busking, we went to see a friend's band and were innocently chillaxing with a Red Stripe and a few shots when he stopped the show and admonished, "No talking during my songs! If you want to talk, go outside."

It made us cringe. To us, gigs are party central; anything goes. But then again, what do we know? Our band was born and raised on the corner of Rat Shit Road and Kick Your Ass Boulevard. The often absurd conditions of our last few hundred shows have carved us into a finely tuned, thick-skinned, musical machine. We've logged in more performance hours than the Doors, Led Zeppelin, and the Beatles combined. Our shows are accompanied by a lullaby of deafening train screeches and the odor of human excrement. We're fresh sushi still squirming on the plate, pure electrical impulse and muscle memory programmed for one thing and one thing only.

Prior to busking, our club crowds mainly consisted of our girl-friends, our devoted cousin Josh, and the bartenders. That was before we set about accumulating fans the hard way: winning them over one at a time. And just as technology had made it possible for us to create a professional-sounding CD without the help of a record label, we had discovered that it also revolutionized the way we promoted.

Before email and the internet, it was an expensive proposition just to advertise an upcoming gig. We had to design and print posters, then spend hours plastering the entire East Village with them, taping them to every payphone, mailbox, bulletin board, and streetlight we could find. Although necessary, it felt more like an act of futility, since an hour after we poster-bombed an area, another band would routinely come along and rip our posters down, making room for their own. We'd have to repeat steps B and C several times before each gig. We were generally looking at a hundred bucks' damage after printing costs just to promote one gig, which would net us half that amount if we were lucky. But in the last decade or so, bands have been able enjoy a level of intimacy and ease of communication with their fans not previously possible.

We had no idea what to expect when we hit the streets in 2003, yet at every show without fail, we religiously displayed an email list sign-up sheet placed conspicuously next to our pile of CDs, and this practice greatly expanded our audiences on the occasions when we surfaced to play a club. We could now reach thousands of Heth-and-Jederz instantly via a one-click email blast or through a simple video blog. And who needs corporate radio when our website radio station streams All Heth and Jed, All the Damn Time? To date, we've accumulated ten thousand names on our email list, each added by a person who walked up and signed under their own volition. I'm proud to say not a single arm was twisted in the process.

THOUGH THE INTERNET levels the playing field and dramatically increased attendance at our club shows, it can still feel like a Herculean feat to be heard above the din of a million bands simultaneously yelling, "Listen to me!" That's why Jed and I make a habit of looking for success anywhere we can find it. Yet, on occasion, it finds us. Like the time a local booking agent who was smitten with our guerilla promotional tactics recommended us to a production company that was scouting every major city for "up and coming" bands. Groups that made the cut would be taped for a live concert television series called *CitySessions*.

We were more than psyched. The shoot was to take place in Times Square's Quad Recording Studios. You know, the building where Tupac was famously shot in the nuts. But as soon as we walked through the studio doors, we were met with the unnerving spectacle of the band ahead of us in a state of complete meltdown. It wasn't hard to miss this fact, especially with the lead singer's shrieks of "*Fuck! Fuck! Fuck!*" being broadcast throughout the studio via its vast array of oversized production monitors adorning every single wall. The unforgiving glare of a fifteen-member crew equipped with state-of-the-art Sony HD cameras had reduced the inexperienced lad to tears.

Noticing Jed's escalating anxiety, I assured him, "Bro, don't worry about those guys. Just 'busk' the gig."

And why the hell not? We had zilch to worry about. Our fingers were more than warmed up from our nonstop street corner touring. When the cameras rolled, we vibrated on our own plane and jammed a killer set. Nine months later, with the concert "in the can," it began airing nationwide on Rave TV. That's when we got a taste of the incredible power of television. Website CD sales spiked every time the concert aired, and people periodically stopped us on the street to say how much they liked the show and to get an autograph.

Then again, the power of television is a double-edged sword. One warm Saturday in the middle of July—the best time to snag tips from folks who are half in the bag—we went prowling for a late-night spot.

But about an hour into the hunt . . . "Jed, dude, what the fuck is going on out here? Where are all these musicians coming from?"

"I don't know man," he replied. "But they sure are everywhere. It's so bizarre."

There were so many musicians, especially in the Union Square station. There was a bagpipe player in our usual spot. A mere sixty feet from him was a lady playing an organ. At the end of the corridor we spied a dude in a furry Elmo costume playing the xylophone, while off in the distance we heard bucket drummers competing for audio space with a flautist who was being overpowered by an electric violinist. With music spewing from every angle, the station sounded like an Ornette Coleman free jazz clusterfuck, making the whole experience feel cheap and corporate, as if buskers had all of a sudden multiplied like the generic Duane Reades or Starbucks now infesting every corner of the city.

Then it dawned on us. *NYC Soundtracks*, a new reality show on MSG network, must be drawing musicians underground in droves. The show was an eight-episode series that featured contestants going head to head in a viewers' choice competition for the best subway busker in all of New York City. We'd auditioned but got no further than a seven-second appearance in the first episode (turned out the producers were looking for solo acts). The lucky winner would be awarded an opening slot at the legendary Beacon Theatre.

All of a sudden, busking was the cool kid on the block. Jed and I had witnessed the cycle before: Whenever a busker seals a movie deal, record deal, or television spot, busking becomes momentarily hip. Still, we knew that in just a few short weeks, the frenzy would die down, and once again, only us stalwart lifers would remain.

Despite the overcrowded conditions, our promotional efforts

inspired new interest from the media when the popular New York City blog Gothamist asked us to write about our busking exploits in a feature called "Tourist (A Tour Diary)." The success of that article became the inspiration for this book, as we continued to jot down informal notes after each gig. At first, we had no idea what our goal was, but little by little, our memoir began taking shape. Next, we threw ourselves into the creation of a sketchy outline and a book proposal. Six months later, we emailed a query letter (a formal letter sent to literary agents, proposing a book idea) to fifty of the biggest literary agents in the country. Within twenty-four hours we had offers from a dozen or so brave souls all willing to represent our magnum opus to publishers—more attention than we'd garnered from the music business in our entire career. It blew our minds, but mostly it said something about how insular the music industry had become. Would they even know talent if they walked by it on the way to work, or if it jammed a hit song for them as they waited for the train? Our earlier prediction had certainly come true: When we took our music to the streets, directly to the people, something had most definitely "come of it."

OUR EXPANDING FAN base and growing popularity underground helped us secure a residency at a short-lived speakeasy called the Apocalypse Lounge on East Third Street and Avenue B in the East Village. It was a throwback to the early '80s downtown art scene, a weekly respite from our otherwise strenuous grind. The club paid homage to New York City's newly resurrected neo-expressionist pop art scene. In keeping with the Warhol Factory theme, there were day-glo collages stuck in every nook of the building, interactive art installations, and even a few genuine Basquiats and Harings hanging on the walls. Since they didn't have a cabaret or liquor license, the set-up was basically illegal, making the scene all the more enjoyable.

We were stoked to discover that all our hard work was paying off in the form of a weekly packed house. Gazing through the neon blue darkness of the front room, we watched like proud parents as wasted European vacationers partied with wasted local kids from Queens and Brooklyn, everyone bonding over our band. This demonstrated two things we'd noticed time and again: Music united the masses, and Heth-and-Jederz were seriously devoted. We were becoming a community rock band. We even printed band t-shirts emblazoned with our new creed: COMMUNITY ROCK, FOR THE PEOPLE BY THE PEOPLE.

The later our sets began, the more surreal the ambience became. A few minutes before our 12 AM slot, I climbed up onto a lumpy carpet that was rolled up against the bar. While ordering, I was momentarily distracted by the silhouette of a naked chick artfully gyrating behind a scrim (the gorgeous goth bartenders took turns stripping between pouring). Despite the fact that I felt the carpet moving underneath me, I ignored my instincts, figuring it was the combination of too much Jimmy Beam and the pre-show jitters. That is, until the Persian rug bucked me off like I was a rodeo cowboy. The next thing I knew, I was lying on the floor with my drink splattered on me, staring up at a smiling face sticking out the end of the rug. The bartender said, "Sorry 'bout that dude. That's just Bob the Human Carpet. He likes when people walk all over him."

Another unusual thing about the place was how one of the employees regularly produced music for Sony Records in a recording studio in the basement. He mentioned he liked our tunes and wanted to invest some cash in us, but word on the street was he was involved with some seriously deranged drug dealers, so we declined as respectfully as possible. Shortly thereafter, he called and said we'd better come over and play him our new songs by midnight or he'd be sending Ramon over . . . whatever the hell that meant. At first we thought he said he'd be sending the Ramones over—which would have been way cooler.

We called his bluff: "Send whoever you want, motherfucker!"
After that they stopped booking us.

DESPITE THE INCREASED turnout, though, we're road weary at club shows and generally about as comfortable as Crocodile Dundee rooming at the Plaza Hotel.

"Hi. Would you mind unlocking the door?" we asked. We were trying to load in for a gig at the Living Room on Ludlow Street.

The huge-ass bouncer responded, "Maybe, if you say please."

"Okay, then," we replied. "Could you please open the fucking door?"

Later we apologized for being a little stressed out. Clearly our patience has been splattered like a rat's brains across the 6 train's third rail, and at times we seem to have misplaced our manners. Still, with so much performance and battle experience percolating under our belts, our confidence in our music has soared. Accordingly, when the sound engineer at that same club was too cool to acknowledge us during sound check, we teased, "Yo, the best fucking band on the East Coast is here!" Then, borrowing a line from Tenacious D, we admonished, "Get ready for us to cum in your ear-pussies!" Good thing we packed the club that night.

The great thing about playing an indoor show is being able to hear each note clearly. All the new songs and riffs we've been developing and straining to hear for the last few months finally come into focus at club shows, as if heard through a sonic microscope. Yet without the occasional train screech or audience meltdown, we feel somewhat out of our element, so we have a little fun goading the audience. If someone bails between songs, we can't refrain from singling them out: "Hey, where you guys going? Don't you like our music? Oh yeah, the Taylor Swift concert is down the block." People seem to like it when a rock band alpha-males the room, becoming the dog whisperers of music. Plus, we'd be remiss if we didn't subvert an uptight atmosphere. Rooted firmly in the school of testing boundaries, à la Jim Morrison and Iggy Pop, we've discovered that the line separating audience from performer is illusory. Holding ourselves apart would be exceedingly elitist; we'll leave that to divas such as the great Céline Dion and her ilk.

At that same show, we tested the club's patience further when they disciplined us in front of all our fans. "Hey, what the fuck are you two doing? You guys can't bring outside beer into the club!"

"Geez, what's the big deal?" we asked.

"Dump that shit out right now, or I'm telling the booker to never let you guys play here again."

Jed and I had to physically restrain most of the bar from kicking the shit out of the club's overzealous security team. We were learning that our fans could be rather protective and that we really, really liked it. No longer was it just my brother and I against the world. We now had allies.

IT'S NOT JUST our attitude toward our audience that differentiates us; while hanging with the other bands before a show, we're usually jealous of the pristine quality of their gear.

"Did you see that guy's guitar, bro? Fuckin' mint!"

"Yeah, dude. Looks like it's never been used."

From daily use, our gear is in a perpetual state of tatters, held together with duct tape and spit. To keep our endless tour rolling along, we faithfully adhere to a daily flight check consisting of morning yoga followed by a test for broken wires, dead strings, and inoperative effect pedals. Notwithstanding moments of envy, we wear our battered gear proudly, like battle scars. After five years in the streets, we've concluded that a band needs to age like a fine wine, and people seem to appreciate the fact we've been knocked around a little. There's simply no substitute for mileage, suffering, and paying your dues. In this age of instant fame, slow-brewed premium rock'n'roll is all the more distinctive.

ONE THING THAT always helps us acclimate to the subway stations after a cushy club show is bullshitting with cool MTA personnel. Many MTA workers, we've found, have a deep affection for the arts. On the whole, they're supportive of subway musicians, treating us like honorary colleagues. Our good buddy Jack Gorski is one of the many subway maintenance guys you see around the stations and has been a loyal friend and supporter for years. Between songs, he often reminisces about the mind-blowing rock shows he experienced in his youth at places like the Fillmore East (now a Chase bank, of course) and Madison Square Garden.

Jack is always in some kind of a tizzy about having to work like a mule. "Garbage cans are supposed to be emptied every two hours but they fill up every sixty minutes! What the fuck are you people putting in here?" he wonders aloud. Another time, he asks, "Did you guys hear that report about subway air quality being safe? Between you and me there's a lot of respiratory issues down here from all the steel dust coming off the metal train wheels. You guys ever seen a greyish-blue cloud hovering in the stations? Whenever the trains brake, that shit kicks up into your lungs."

"Makes sense, man. Lately Jed and I have been feeling like a couple of coal miners. When we get home after a day of singing, we blow our noses and out comes a river of black soot."

After one of our shows, Jack slammed the garbage can shut and remarked, "Sounds like you guys are going through a Zeppelin phase. You kind of have that Jimmy Page thing going on, and I should know 'cause I've seen them seven times!"

"No fucking way! You saw them live?"

"Yup! At the Garden and Nassau."

We mentioned how we'd been receiving weekly emails with comments like, "Your music reminds me of all the great times tailgating with my childhood friends."

Jack spoke about practically growing up at the Fillmore and CBGB. "Ever been in the bathroom at CB's? Gross or what?"

"Yeah gross, but we loved it."

"Hang on. I got something in my locker to show you guys."

He returned with a photo album packed with faded Polaroids, a veritable time capsule of classic New York City rock history. There were front-row snapshots of seminal groups like the New York Dolls, the Damned, and Patti Smith in their heyday. He also had shots of more mainstream groups like Uriah Heep, Bad Company, Boston, Skynyrd, and Thin Lizzy.

Just then, Mushroom, the dude who grows shrooms in hundred-gallon fish tanks in his Astoria basement, mystically happened upon the party.

"Hey dudes. How's it going?"

"Cool man! What's going on?"

"Well for one thing, I have a new crop of primo fungi coming in and they are looking pretty sweet. I'm saving you boys some very nice caps and stems. But please, promise me you'll never eat them raw. Okay? Only make tea."

"No problem," we replied. "Scout's honor."

Mush was our Captain Trips, having never met a drug he didn't like. Might be why all his teeth were AWOL . . . too much meth?

"Hey man, allow me to introduce you to our good friend Jack."

"Nice to meet you," Mush said, fiddling with his dentures. The two surveyed each other with the quizzical looks of long lost brothers. After shaking hands, they perused Jack's awesome photo collection only to realize they'd both attended many of the same concerts over thirty years ago. The pièce de résistance came when Jack ran to his locker yet again, this time returning with a sleeveless denim jacket. "Check it out." The backside was painted with a flawless rendition of the cover art for Led Zeppelin's *Houses of the Holy*.

"Holy shit!" we all agreed.

"I paid some kid twenty bucks to paint it back in 1975."

"Damn!" Mushroom said. "That thing should be hanging in the Louvre."

14

Future Memory

[JED]

ver since that fateful night at Panna II, Heth and I had been on
an uninterrupted rock'n'roll bender, struggling to get this family
business of ours off the ground. Six years in, we were starting
to feel like we might have overdone it a little. We were battle-
weary, punch-drunk, and practically sleepwalking through gigs like
bleary-eyed zombies. Heth's asthma was acting up and I'd been
enjoying the wonderment of chronic nasal infections, all symptoms
of working constantly without much fresh air or a vacation. We'd
lost our perspective, and inspiration was seriously on the wane.

One day not too long ago, in desperate need of a recharge and
a home-cooked meal, we headed over to Penn Station to catch
the Dover Midtown Direct and make the forty-five minute trip to
Mom's apartment in Jersey.

On that rare day off it's always a relief to travel the city with
only a gigantic coffee in hand, free from the two hundred pounds
of musical baggage we're used to dragging all over God's creation.
Sometimes it even feels like we're attending a party in our honor.
The formerly cold and lonely subway corridors are now filled with
Heth-and-Jederz and fellow buskers! Along the way, we're met by

smiling faces, people excited to run into us, calling out, "All right, Heth and Jed! How's it going, guys?" "Hey! What's up?" we smile back, forever blown away when we get the royal treatment.

As soon as we hopped off the N train at Thirty-fourth Street, on our way to Penn Station, a rocker-in-training wearing a rad Lamb of God shirt and dark shades threw the devil's horns our way. "Hey, you guys fucking rock!" he called out. "I mean it, you fucking rock!"

We threw two hands in the air to shoot him back a respectable double dose of hornage.

There's nothing more gratifying than being acknowledged, yet on the train ride out to Mom's all we could think about was the quiet lushness of our old childhood retreat, St. Phil's woods.

"Dude, we gotta go there today," Heth said, eager to hug a tree.

Mom met us at the train station. Despite her frequent grumblings that she's overdue for a face-lift, she looks great. For the last couple years, she's been sporting a magnificent kinky perm. It's so distinctive it often elicits comments like "you go, girl!" from people who think it's natural. She's as feisty as ever, too—still loves her TV shows and is an expert at handling both the newfangled FIOS remote and her 60" LCD flat screen, given to her by her brother on her seventy-second birthday. God forbid one of us tries to commandeer that hardware; she's selective about what she watches. In particular, if George Bush, Jr. comes on the screen, she totally loses it. "Turn that channel right now! I already told you, that man is not allowed in this house!"

"All right, all right Mom! Settle down."

In retirement, she'd also reclaimed a sizeable chunk of her artistic side, having begun a series of very large paintings. Perhaps taking a cue from us, Mom has even become a busker of sorts, drumming up the courage to hawk her Pollock-esque works at North Jersey street festivals.

After stuffing ourselves silly with one of her signature meals (*boeuf bourguignon* cooked to perfection), we prepared for our pilgrimage to the woods of yore by digging around on the interwebs a bit. Who was this St. Philomena, anyway?

"Patron saint of children?" Heth crowed, skimming the Wikipedia page. "That's crazy! She definitely watched over us."

"Duh," I replied. "Why else do you think we're still alive?"

ON SCENE, we instinctively gravitated to one of our former access routes, the one we'd used as kids, but the entryway to our childhood oasis was overgrown with thorny tangles of ivy and weeds. So we clawed and stomped our way through the jungle until our inner GPS units synchronized, pointing us in the direction of the most sacred spot of all: The logs. Time to pay our respects to the old stomping grounds.

I closed my eyes and took a deep breath. The sunrays filtering through the dense canopy of maples flickered across my face. The air was extra sweet from a recent rainfall, and the trees that unfailingly balanced and insulated us from cops and family drama greeted us like old friends. They'd grown taller and their trunks had thickened with age, and some had even spawned children of their own.

Amid tiny shards of decaying logs, Heth found a crusty Old Milwaukee beer can. He flicked off a giant daddy longlegs and held the can up to the sunlight for further inspection.

"Holy crap! It's got the old logo from the '80s. I bet Ed threw it there."

After that, we couldn't help but play a round or two of "remember when." We rapped about how far we'd come since the last time we'd stood in this exact spot smoking Bill's testicle-scented weed, dreaming of rock'n'roll stardom.

"You know, it just wasn't the right time for Airport Hug," I suggested. "We had all the potential to be a great band but just couldn't get any traction."

"Whataya talking about?" Heth countered. "We *were* a great band. Just had too much baggage and not enough luck. And what if we'd made it? Would you have liked being cooped up in a tour bus smelling Drake's farts for the rest of your natural life?"

I had to concede the point.

"You know, maybe we're not rich and famous," Heth said, "but we've definitely lived a rich life."

"Oh no. Here we go," I said half-jokingly. I knew he was going to hit me with one of his philosophical diatribes.

"We're full-time musicians, man! Can you fucking believe that? And we've been on a totally kick-ass journey together!"

I think we ultimately owed the resurrection of our brotherhood to Mom, who always encouraged us to look out for one another. As kids, we had no idea what she was talking about when she drilled into our brains, "Never let anything come between you two!"

"Do you think Dad's proud of us?" Heth suddenly asked me.

"I don't know," I replied, as honestly as I could; it's been so many years since we've spoken. In early 2009 at one of our Forty-second Street Times Square shows, while we were knee-deep in a toe-curling jam for an audience of over two hundred people, who should emerge from behind a white metal column but Dad. He was grooving to the scene, sizing up the crowd while staring at us, teary-eyed. Without saying a word he walked over, grabbed a few of our CDs, and left without paying.

"One thing's for sure," I said. "He definitely developed our musical palette . . . turning us on to jazz and classical at such an early age. But maybe that's why we gravitated to the raw power of three-chord rock."

Either way, we credit him with instilling the spirit of defiance that keeps us going even in the face of defeat.

It was getting dark when we finally bailed, but we couldn't leave without making a lap around 32 Lex for old time's sake. Our folks had sold it a few years prior, and by then, we had already grown to dread our occasional visits. Two seconds inside those walls was all it took for us to revert to old childhood patterns, eternally rehashing some unresolved, unimportant bullshit. It didn't matter how long ago they once raged, the energy-presence of a million and one lingering battles just wouldn't fade.

"Hope the new owners smudged the place or performed a séance before moving in," Heth said.

"Maybe it'll accidentally catch fire . . ." I joked.

The day the movers had split from 32 Lex with the last bit of Mom's furniture, our good buddy Mike—the brains behind inserting the porn spread in my trumpet lesson book—had dropped by to document one final walk-through. Rather than bidding goodbye to an old friend, ridding ourselves of our old house had felt more like finally taking off a pair of circulation-destroying, sperm count–annihilating skinny jeans.

The video shows us descending into our moldy basement for the last time. Serving as official videographer, Mike asks, "Heth, isn't this where you learned how to play drums?"

"Yeah. This is where I spent like six weeks figuring out Rush's *Moving Pictures*. My Rototoms were positioned somewhere right about . . . here," Heth says, proudly air drumming the intro to "YYZ." *Bah, duh bah bah bah, duh bah bah bah bah!*

The camera focuses on the laundry room. I ask, "Hey Mike, isn't that where you banged Cindy Friedman at one of our first keg parties?"

Laughing. "Yup, her head kept smacking into the ironing board."

"Mike," I tell him, "you're such a romantic, dude!"

IT WAS A steamy Friday night when, feeling rejuvenated, we hopped a train back to the city. We didn't have one of our Music Under New York scheduled shows, but we needed to rock, so we collected our gear and headed out in search of an unauthorized spot. First we swung by Penn Station with hopes of jamming in the air conditioning while chugging a few beers, but no such luck. Next we headed downtown to sweltering Union Square where, surprisingly, none of our brethren were performing. We moved in and staked our claim.

We went through the familiar checklist of setting up, opening our guitar case, optimistically positioning it front and center for tips. Funny how after a thousand shows, we still get butterflies. A train screeched into the station and with the throbbing mass of humanity flooding all around us, we flicked on our amps. The light by the power switch glowed yellow. All systems go.

Heth announced, "This one's called 'Future Memory.'"

We looked at each other and nodded.

"Let's rock!"

> *A future memory*
> *Of where I'm gonna be*
> *If things work out*
> *You standing next to me.*
>
> *You're way before your time,*
> *You're so special*
> *And there's no doubt*
> *You'll be standing next to me.*

ACKNOWLEDGMENTS

Thanks to our agent Andrea Somberg at the Harvey Klinger Literary Agency for believing in us and selling our book. Special thanks to our editor Anne Horowitz and the wonderful people at Soft Skull Press/ Counterpoint. Gratitude abounding to producer Jamie Candiloro and to our good buds Michelle Goodman, Greta Brinkman, Linda Burnside, Joe Salerno, Janice Muscio, and Susan Romweber, who helped organize our muddled mess of a first draft. To the folks at Music Under New York for giving us a musical home. To the City of New York and the Metropolitan Transit Authority for supplying the real estate upon which to rock, and to the people of New York City for supporting us,

To Mom, who helped us dig into the past, and to Hope, Larry Masser, Milo, Jack, and Rocket for their love and support. To Mike Lonoff for being a great friend and for reminding us of many early stories. Thanks to Ed's room alumni, wherever you may be.

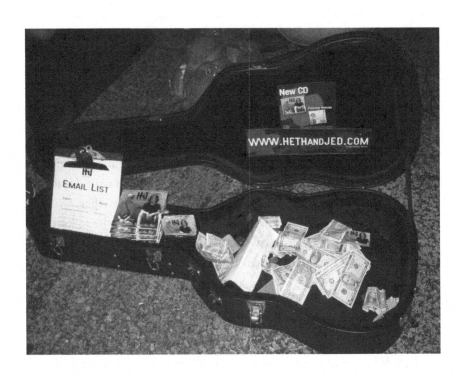

Printed in the United States
by Baker & Taylor Publisher Services